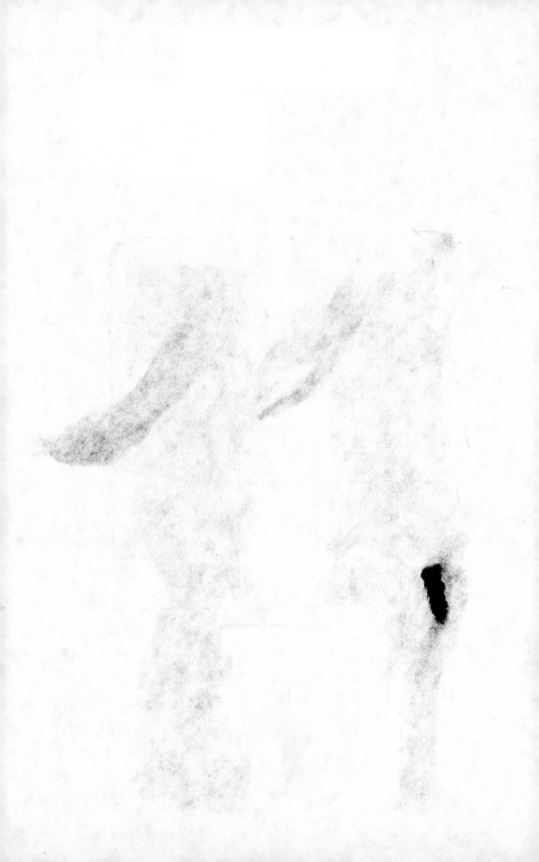

Waddling to War on LST 834
The Ventures and Adventures of a Skylarking Sailor in World War II

Bob Shannon

authorHOUSE™

1663 LIBERTY DRIVE, SUITE 200
BLOOMINGTON, INDIANA 47403
(800) 839-8640

First published by AuthorHouse 12/06/05

ISBN: 1-4208-6549-8 (sc)

Library of Congress Control Number: 2005910734

Printed in the United States of America
Bloomington, Indiana

This book is printed on acid-free paper.

Chapter One
A Bit of Preambling

Of the sixteen million people who served in the United States military during World War II, few could have been as ill prepared for the experience as me. Nonetheless, at age eighteen, off I went to war. American kids like me lost their provincialism in a hurry. Young men who had never seen an ocean or been on the water in anything bigger than a rowboat became highly proficient seamen, knowledgeable in the ways of war, effective in combat. Boys quickly acquired the skills and savvy in specializations completely unknown to them before entering the Navy. They were possibilists, pragmatists. "If it works, it's good," became their modus operandi, the principle they relied on. Luck was a factor they learned to regard with awe and respect. Being the fickle factor, luck dealt these novice seamen the good and the bad, handing out life-saving and life-destroying events indiscriminately, whimsically. I, too, became attuned to these realities.

For two years I was a sailor, twenty-three months and sixteen days, traveling half-way round the world to war at Okinawa. I was not good at sailoring, not serious about the Navy or the tasks I was to perform. But because of, or maybe in spite of, a lack of seriousness, I collected a million memorable experiences that have stayed with me. These experiences are the text for this story.

Chapter Two
The Folly and Foolishness of Boot Camp

A raw recruit, I was in no position to know that what we did each day in Boot Camp was based on a set of assumptions that were essentially self-contradictory. Intuitively, I concluded that what we were doing had nothing to do with what I would be doing if I were at sea. That did not require much intelligence or intuition. But, I could never assume that my judgment was reliable. I had to assume that the daily grind was okay, part of the process. Anyway, crazy as it now seems, I rather enjoyed the game.

Every day we did close-order drill. That is, we marched. The old left right, left right, to the rear march, to the rear march, left flank march, right flank march, halt one two. Then a few more to the rear march just to get it right. Everyone was bitching about it. "Why," we asked, "are we doing this?" On what premise would those who fashion the essentials of recruit training deduce that lots of close-order drill was imperative to our development for life at sea? Discipline? Yes, they surmised, extensive participation in close order drill makes for a well-disciplined sailor. Such nonsense.

And so it went. Everyone went to the rifle range to develop some proficiency in shooting a rifle. That was the only time I saw a rifle during my Navy days or after. We had a horrible day learning to fight an oil fire. What a mess that was. Thank heavens it was a one time experience. One day we all had to box. Matched against some fellow about my size, I tied on the gloves and had a go at boxing. Why? Don't ask. Running the obstacle course was a daily event. Another day we marched to the gas chamber, were handed a gas mask, ushered into the gas chamber and told to put on the gas mask. When the chamber was full of tear gas we were told to remove the gas mask and then put it back on. A one shot experience. But so what? Why?

Day after day we sat in classrooms viewing films on venereal disease, with close-up photos of diseased, warty, scabby penises. Pitiful sights. I wonder if those films kept anyone from visiting the world's brothels.

Airplane recognition classes were the most frequent, and the most boring, useless endeavors ever contrived. The objective was the education of all sailors in knowing, in a fraction of a second, the differences between a Japanese airplane and a U. S. airplane. It did not work. But, some influential persons insisted that it did work. So, we did it.

In Boot Camp we were required to roll our trousers, wrinkle free, and tie them with six inch cords. This is the way sailors of ancient days did it, so we were required to do it. A silly endeavor with no practical consequence other than to pass inspections in Boot Camp. Nothing hooked up.

Oddly enough, I actually enjoyed Boot Camp. Perhaps it was nothing more than being away from home, somewhat on my own. But, too, each day contained some new experience...not necessarily a good experience, but something new in my life. Most events were a one time thing, other than the infernal marching. Being a one time event meant that once it was finished, that was that, check it off the list. Now what? Hardly anything called for thinking. Maybe that's why I liked it. Several of my high school chums were with me, too. That helped. None of us knew what we were doing, but we were at a carefree, worry free moment in life, certain that nothing could hurt us. Only the other guys need worry.

On the first day we were herded into a huge room and everyone was given a cardboard box. Then came the command. "Remove your clothing, everything. Put your clothing in the box, seal it, address it to the home you left behind." Minutes later I stood with one hundred sixty raw recruits, all of us buck naked, in possession of absolutely nothing. Now what?

We formed a single line and entered the next room for measuring and labeling. Each man was measured and marked for shoes, hat, uniforms, trouser length, arms, neck. With each measurement a number was scribbled somewhere on the naked body. On to the next room.

In the next room the baffling humiliation continued. Bam! Something struck me in the chest. "Don't just stand there sailor, open that mattress cover and keep moving." I did as directed and followed the guy in front of me. Items bounced off my chest and into the mattress cover. Expertise at this maneuver was instantly acquired. It became a contest between me and the guy doing the tossing, a do or die circumstance. Socks, shoes, underwear, blue jeans, shirts, uniforms, hats, canvas puttees, towels, soap dish, razor, sea bag, duffel bag, pea coat, neckerchief, and a copy of the Blue Jackets Manual...Everything I would need in my new life. On to the next room.

I dragged the mattress cover through the door in time to hear, "Okay sailors, the uniform of the day is undress blues and puttees. Git yourself into uniform and haul yourself and your gear over to barracks 809 on C Street."

What in the world is this guy talking about? Undress blues? Puttees? I looked around the room, searching for someone who understood. Some seemed to know. I sorted through the mess in my mattress cover, fishing out clothing, pulling it on my aching body, gradually getting dressed in the uniform of the day. Then, ready to go, I tried to lift the sea bag filled with my new life style. God, was it heavy. Managing that bagful (or did the bagful manage me) as the struggle for survival of the fittest. Ultimately I made it to the barracks, dragged myself upstairs and to a bunk. That was Boot Camp.

There is no place to hide in the Navy. Everyone and everything is visible. One's peculiarities, eccentricities, idiosyncrasies become evident in a hurry. It was impossible to escape the presence of everyone in the group now known as Company 1309. The boys of 1309 were never out of sight, nor me out of their sight. Night and day, every twenty-four hours, we were together, together, together. That part I grew to dislike. But there were some comical events that occurred because of the incessant togetherness. Marion Weakly was one of those comical events. That name is not an invention. Marion Weakly was his name and his story gives good reason to suspect its authenticity. His name takes on an incredible poignancy. Marion assumed the role of company tough guy. He tried desperately to cast himself in that role, exhibiting a kind of bravado, a swagger.

Whenever Company 1309 marched anywhere Marion Weakly managed to get himself designated as the one to call cadence, to march alongside the company calling cadence in a gruff, he-man style. He loved it.

One day we marched off to get some inoculations, our first shots. Weakly called cadence, played the hot dog, led us to the building where we were to receive the shots. We were scheduled for two shots and a vaccination. Several other companies were there for the same treatment so the line of recruits was long. The day was hot. The line moved along very slowly. Once inside the building we could see the pharmacist mates (better known as pecker checkers) far across the room giving the shots and the vaccinations. Hundreds of neophyte sailors reluctantly progressed toward their fate. There were the customary admonitions and jokes bantered about regarding the severity of these shots, how much they hurt, and how they were nothing compared to what we were in for the next week when we would get the shot of all shots, the one where you get the square needle in the left testicle. When he got near to the medics' table and his turn for the shots, Marion Weakly began to cry. Poor Weakly,

9

couldn't hold back. Visibly trembling, the tough guy was in tears.

That was it for Weakly. Everyone gave him the business, made fun

of him unmercifully. Sobbing uncontrollably, Weakly whimpered,

"Damn you guys, you ain't got no right makin' fun of me. I ain't

New Recruit in Boot Camp

never had no shots in my whole life." From that moment on, Weakly

was the company joke, the butt of relentless teasing for the duration

of Boot Camp. He relinquished his role as the big shot and never

again sought to call cadence. Marion Weakly, the weakling.

Before entering the Navy I had never shaved. There was nothing to shave. No whiskers. How I envied the bristles on the chins of my buddies. A little fuzz was the extent of my facial hair. My Navy issue razor was a black plastic affair that came in three pieces. One night, just for the hell of it, I put the razor together, lathered, and shaved. Afterward, peering into the mirror, I saw that the fuzz on my chin was still there. So much for shaving. That was the night before our first Saturday morning inspection.

Saturday morning in Boot Camp was inspection time, known to all as Captain's Inspection. I don't think a fellow with the rank of captain ever inspected us. Nevertheless, it was labeled Captain's Inspection. Everything and every individual was inspected. It was serious business. No laughing matter, even though the entire routine was laughable. We mustered on the parade grounds in a spotless white uniform. That is, as spotless as one could get the uniform, scrubbing it by hand with a bar of soap and a scrub brush. Part of the game called inspection was to stand in formation in the hot sun waiting for the "Captain" and his party of inspectors to arrive. The waiting period was passed standing at "parade rest," a reasonably

11

comfortable position with feet apart and hands clasped behind the back. When the command "attention" was barked, that meant that the inspection party had arrived. Invariably, a few recruits would begin to weave about, subsequently collapse onto the pavement in a faint, and then be hauled off to a bed at the base hospital, thereby escaping the heat and the inspection. Those faintings were especially numerous if Saturday morning inspection followed a Friday afternoon inoculation.

The inspecting "captain" would stroll up and down rows of roasting recruits, pausing occasionally to criticize some aspect of a fellow's appearance. During the first one of these Saturday shindigs the inspecting officer halted in front of me. He examined my chin, tugged on one of those whiskers I had failed to remove. "Son, when did you shave?" he asked. "Last night, Sir. I tried to anyway," I replied. "Well, you better try it again." He moved on down the line.

That night I was at the sink preparing to try shaving for the second time. Clancy, a fellow from home, was at the adjacent sink. He showed me that I had put the razor together upside down, making it impossible for the blade to function. He put it together properly. I shaved and the whiskers miraculously disappeared. How dumb can you get?

After weeks of marching, tear gas drills, fire fighting, viewing slides of Japanese airplanes, scrubbing clothes by hand, mess duty, inoculations against every disease known to man, viewing movies showing pimpled penises on victims of venereal disease, firing rifles, taking standardized tests, interviews with specialists who asked profound question such as "Do you like girls?", inspections, boxing, obstacle courses…Boot Camp at last came to an end. We even got paid. Eighty dollars for eight weeks. Big money. I put on the dress blue uniform and marched to the train with my buddies singing, "Happy is the day when the Navy gets its pay, and we go rolling rolling home." We were salty sailors heading home for an eight day leave.

Chapter Three
Camp Bradford

Camp Bradford at Virginia Beach, Virginia, was a good illustration of how military minds can turn a beautiful setting into a horrible place. Virginia Beach had long been the proud possessor of a fine reputation earned during peaceful years of civilian planning and occupancy. Consequently, we were delighted to leave the Midwest on a troop train heading for this internationally renowned seaside community. Boy oh boy, did we have it wrong.

Camp Bradford, Virginia had been literally carved out of the land. The camp consisted of sand, asphalt, quonset huts, hundreds of tent-like barracks structures, and a lovely beach front on the sea. The entire base had an aura of temporariness. It seemed that the whole place could disappear any moment, swallowed up by sand. It was in this setting that three fundamental decisions were made that impacted significantly on my life. Some foolishness became part of the scene, beginning with standing guard duty.

The idea of guarding something unguardable could only make sense to a military mind. It was the ultimate absurdity, but was all pervasive in the Navy of World War II. Everyone was required to stand guard duty now and then while at Camp Bradford. There was nothing on the base that actually needed guarding. No secret documents, no high level leaders, no super secret specialized armament or equipment. Only sand, tents, quonset huts, and garbage cans. Nonetheless, we all stood guard duty from time to time. That's when I met Fitzpatrick.

One night I had the misfortune of being selected to stand guard duty on the midnight to 4:00 A.M. watch. So was Fitzpatrick. I reported to a quonset hut that was headquarters of the base Shore Patrol, and the place where guard duty assignments were made. Fifteen or twenty guard duty assignees stood waiting. A big fellow; red hair, freckle-faced, nose as big and red as mine, stood beside me.

Fitzpatrick was his name. Each of us was issued a forty-five caliber pistol in a leather holster attached to a belt. It was the standard weapon issued to anyone "doing" guard duty. I buckled the pistol around my waist just like I knew what I was doing. I confided to Fitzpatrick that I did not know how to use the gun. He said, "Don't worry about it. Just keep it in the holster. It's safer that way. The forty-five is just for show." I never forgot his advice. There were many, many times that I had guard duty aboard ship, but I never took the gun out of the holster, never in the two years I spent in the Navy.

When assignments for guard duty were called out I learned that Fitzpatrick and I were designated a team responsible for patrolling an area know as Queens. That meant nothing to me, but it did to Fitzpatrick. He blurted, "Jesus man, why the hell are you sending us to Queens? That's way out where Christ lost his shoes." The response to Fitzpatrick was predictable. "That's tough shit sailor. Now git goin'. I'll be comin' by in the jeep to see how you are gettin' along."

That night I found out where Christ lost his shoes. Fitzpatrick and I guarded a bunch of garbage cans and he kept me laughing until 4:00 A.M. I never saw him again. I wish I had asked him more about Christ losing his shoes.

Chapter Four
An All Male Society

In mid-August 1944, one hundred and fifteen men were plucked from the sands of Virginia Beach and told that they were to become a new, self-contained, all male society. I was one of them. We were to live on an island. The island, heretofore uninhabited, was three hundred twenty-eight feet long and fifty feet wide, and it was movable. Slowly, nonetheless movable. The movable island, a Landing Ship Tank, would be found in the Ohio River near Pittsburgh, Pennsylvania.

Determining who would be in a particular crew was a simple matter for those in charge of such things at Camp Bradford. You need 115, simply lop off that many. But, deciding what each individual would be trained to do aboard the new ship required making some perfunctory assessments of individual competence. It was a slapdash procedure. Based on very little knowledge or evidence, decisions were made as to who would be trained to do what aboard ship. While the system amounted to little more than pulling names out of a hat, it was unavoidable. Scores made on standardized tests we had taken in Boot Camp followed us to Camp Bradford. Based on those test scores and a brief interview, it was determined that I would become a radarman. I could have been designated as a trainee signalman, storekeeper, yeoman, radioman, machinist mate, gunner's mate, shipfitter, cook, baker, coxswain, quartermaster, or anything else required to perform the manifold tasks on a Landing Ship Tank. I was deemed a proper candidate for operating the radar equipment. So, off I went to radar school. I didn't have the faintest idea what radar was, but my assignment turned out to be a lucky punch.

For part of the radar schooling I was sent to the Cavalier Hotel on Virginia Beach for what turned out to be a wonderful period. Before the war the Cavalier had been a premier resort hotel. The

Navy had taken over the hotel to use in training radio and radar personnel. They must have retained the chefs from pre-war days. Meals were first-rate. Fresh fruits and vegetables, several choices of meats, fancy cakes and pies. It was unbelievable. And we ate at small tables in a proper dining room. Possibly I learned something about radar during that week, but the most significant thing I learned in that elegant setting was that I wanted to see a whole lot more of that life style. One taste of living at the Cavalier and I was hooked.

Liberty was an every night privilege during my time at the Cavalier. No liberty passes were necessary. The fence at the rear of the hotel had an enormous opening in it. One simply put on a dress uniform, walked through the gaping hole in the fence, and went off to town for the evening. No restrictions or checks on going out or coming in. No shore patrols. No nothing. Such suffering.

Back at Camp Bradford following my brief stint at the luxury hotel, the days focused on activities with the men I would live with on the 834 and learning more about operation of radar equipment. Every aspect of it was new to me. Anything electronic was foreign to anything in my experience. The vocabulary, the scientific principles, the technology, and rudiments of operating the equipment, the whole

deal had me befuddled. Instructors were of little help. They were

both unskilled and uneducated as teachers. Instruction manuals

provided some help. Learning how to operate the radar was, as it is

in learning most anything, a trial and error process, a do it yourself

kit. I stumbled along, hiding my ignorance, avoiding situations

where my ineptness would be evident.

Afternoons were devoted to nonsensical activities with the

entire crew. Perhaps the intent was for officers and crew to begin

to get acquainted, to learn to function as a unit. Or maybe we

were just killing time while waiting for construction of our ship

to be completed. But the stuff we did was sheer nonsense. More

marching, more slides of Japanese airplanes, more films on venereal

disease. Looking at slides of Japanese and American airplanes

was real folly, just as it had been in Boot Camp. The objective of

the exercise, presumably, was to teach us to distinguish between

a Japanese airplane and an American airplane so we would know

which planes to destroy and which planes to welcome. I never

became capable of sorting out one airplane from another. When we got into the thick of things, into the actual business of shooting down airplanes, I discovered that no one else had learned to distinguish between a Japanese airplane and an American airplane. The impact of the movies about venereal disease was another matter. They were impressive. I have never forgotten those films of disease ridden, pimply, scabby, warty penises. But what good did they do? The thousands of sailors heading into Norfolk or any other city paid no heed to those vivid film portrayals of the hazards of sex. The films were fascinating, but so were the brothels and all the honeys hanging around the bars and street corners. Once Eros the Mischief Maker took charge, all precautionary measures went out the window. One popular rationalization for a sailor's promiscuity (as well as that of the female population) during World War II was, "Why not? I'll probably be dead in a short time." That principle became the justification for doing most anything one wanted to do. No doubt the same rationalization has prevailed throughout history.

Norfolk, Virginia has been a Navy town ever since the American Revolution. During World War II the city was wall to wall sailors day and night, seven days a week. Even so, I had a great time in

Norfolk. What I learned on liberty may not have been profound, but it certainly was basic training in the stuff and staff of life. The first of those weekends in Norfolk is particularly memorable.

I went into town with four or five of my new shipmates. First stop was the burlesque show. It was my first burlesque show, my introduction to the intoxicating world of a stage full of bare boobs. Our seats were in the front row. Right there in front of me, a stage full of scantily clad, long legged, bare bosomed dancing girls, their delicious breasts bouncing beautifully to the throbbing beat of music played by the pit band. Ecstasy! Airplane recognition I never mastered, but one take of that burlesque show stayed with me for a lifetime.

After the show we wandered the streets of Norfolk and happened onto two of our shipmates, Tony Danapas and John Penn. With them was a floozy, Tony's girlfriend for the night. Tony Danapas was a character. He was one of the few men in our newly formed crew who had some experience at sea. Consequently, Tony had already been named chief boatswain's mate. Stupid, arrogant, and crude, Tony possessed all of the essential attributes for the job. Tony walked with a swagger. He inserted obscenities into every phrase he uttered. In civilian life he had worked as a sponge diver out of Tarpon Springs, Florida. He and I disliked each other at first sight and we sustained that mutual disdain throughout our time on the 834. But, John Penn was a delightful fellow. He was eighteen, a comical, venturesome guy who was destined to crowd a lot of mischievous living into his Navy experience. John was clever enough to recognize that cultivating a cozy relationship with the chief boatswain's mate would serve him well. He flattered Tony and quickly became his protégé. It was a smart move on John's part. Danapas, in addition to his other obnoxious characteristics, was a loud, yuk yuk sort of a guy. When we met that night in Norfolk, Tony went through a few yuk yuks, introduced us to his girlfriend, and said to her, "Honey, tell the boys what you are going to do to Penn if he don't shape up." She said, "Ah'm gonna bounce his ass against the bulkhead." Tony roared out his yuk yuk yuks with gusto and said, "Now ain't she really somethin'? Ain't she?" That was it. The three of them walked on down the street. We went in the opposite direction. Tony was to become the central figure in many fiascoes aboard the 834.

While I was engaged in the battle of Camp Bradford on the Virginia shore, decisions were made that would significantly affect my life and the lives of hundreds of thousands of other men and women. Between September 29 and October 1, 1944, Admiral Nimitz, Admiral King, Admiral Spruance, General Buckner, and General Harmon met in a top floor suite at the St. Francis Hotel in San Francisco. The suite belonged to the widow of a principal owner of Pope and Talbot Shipbuilders. She had loaned her place to the Navy for the duration of the war. High ranking military men seemed to be adept at acquiring lush living quarters for themselves. For me and my peers a tent in the sand was considered appropriate. For Admiral Nimitz it was a suite at the St. Francis. Ah, for the perquisites of rank. The five military leaders came together to formulate the specifics of a plan for extending the war in the Pacific. There were some major disagreements on which islands should become targeted for invasion. Admiral King advocated invasion of Formosa. The others, perhaps because of the influence of General MacArthur, favored hitting Luzon in the Philippines. Their deliberations resulted in the plan which became known as Operation Iceberg. It specified

25

invasion of Luzon on December 20, 1944, Iwo Jima on January 20, 1945, and Okinawa March 1, 1945. At that moment, Okinawa began to figure in my destiny.

"Now hear this! Muster tomorrow morning, 0700, packed and ready to go. We will depart immediately for Pittsburgh, Pennsylvania." That announcement was received with much back-slapping and cheering. Everyone had had far too much of Camp Bradford and Norfolk. Pittsburgh sounded good, even though it was a new place for almost the entire crew. Perhaps that's what made the idea so attractive—the newness of it all.

For a guy in a Navy uniform in 1944, Pittsburgh was paradise. There were very few sailors around. And what made the situation even better is that Carnegie Tech University was our headquarters. A residence hall on the Carnegie Tech campus became our barracks building. What a transition. One day the sand of Camp Bradford was home. Next day, the pastoral setting of a beautiful college campus was home. No marching, no morning muster. Just a casual stroll across the tree lined campus to meals in the university dining hall. And liberty every night. Pittsburgh was among the best towns in the United States for a sailor on liberty during World War II. Every day there were notes on the bulletin board in our residence hall: "Wanted, seven sailors for a party tonight at 8:00 P. M. Please telephone." We were in heaven.

Our responsibilities while in Pittsburgh were virtually nonexistent. Each day we were bused out to the shipyard where final phases of work on the LST 834 were being completed. It was almost ready for launching. Our contribution was to get in the way of the shipyard workers who were trying to complete the job on schedule.

Launching of the 834 took place the second week we were in Pittsburgh, October 20, 1944. There was no christening in the style accorded a ship like the Queen Mary or the battleship Missouri, but we did have a sponsor, Mrs. Harold Oberg. We stood at attention during a brief ceremony, then watched our ship slide down the ways and splash into the Ohio River. It floated. Amen. The folks at the American Bridge Company Shipyard had done well.

Chapter Five
LST 834 -- Why Did She Happen?

The LST, Landing Ship Tank, was born and bred during World War II. Impetus for the creation of this large sea-going amphibious craft came from the British experience at Dunkirk in 1940. To rescue the thousands of British troops trapped on the beaches at Dunkirk every kind of boat or ship that could go near to or onto the beach was put into action. The situation was desperate. Troops were facing certain annihilation or capture by the Germans. The experience taught the British Admiralty that a large amphibious ship was essential to making future assaults and invasions of the continent. In November, 1941 representatives of the British Admiralty met with some members of the United States Bureau of Ships to develop plans for creating the proposed warship. John Niedermair of the U.S Bureau of Ships quickly put together a basic design. Some modifications were made, of course, but the Niedermair design became the fundamental one for construction of 1,051 LSTs during World War II. Because all of the coastal shipyards were involved in construction of deep-draft ships, inland steel fabrication yards located on principal rivers, primarily the Ohio River, were converted to shipyards for the construction of the LST. As expertise in construction evolved, the giant ships were being completed in only two months time, an incredible accomplishment.

Our ship was constructed at the American Bridge Company Shipyard, Ambridge, Pennsylvania. In the days following launching I did a lot of exploring, nosing about the new ship. Examining the endless compartments was an awesome, exhilarating experience. Every hatchway I passed through revealed something fascinating, something new. Although the LST was the ugly duckling of the Navy, deservedly acquiring the sobriquet "Large Slow Target," to me, a kid as green as grass, the ship was fabulous. In terms of the amphibious vessels, the LST was the biggest. From bow to stern it was 328 feet long and it had a 50-foot beam. Two diesel-powered propellers kept us going, but even at flank speed it is doubtful that the 834 could do twelve knots. Armament consisted of two twin and four single 40mm anti-aircraft guns and 12-20mm anti-aircraft guns. A huge tank deck and bow doors were the unique aspects of the LST.

LST 834 launched at Pittsburgh

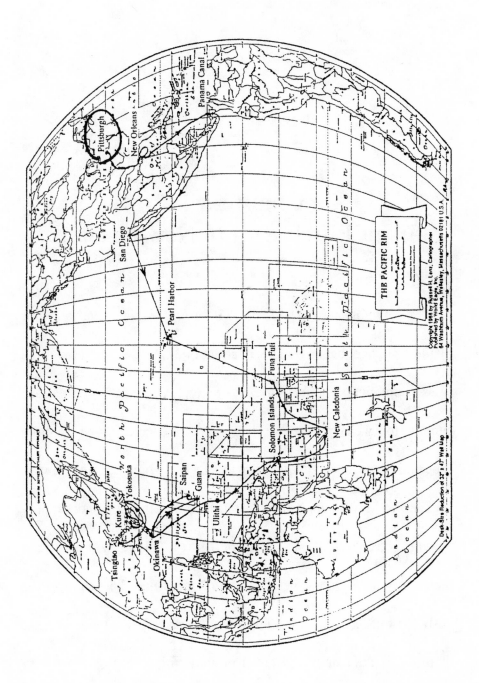

Chapter Six
From Pittsburgh to New Orleans

On November 10, 1944, the 834 was commissioned and our maiden voyage began. The destination? Down the Ohio and Mississippi rivers to New Orleans. A ferry crew and a temporary captain took charge for the trip down the rivers. Navigating, especially into and out of the many locks, demanded real savvy, specialized knowledge and experience, commodities in short supply among the rookies that made up our crew. The ferry crew was a bunch of combat tough veterans who had earned their right to the cushy task of ferrying new ships down the rivers. Most every one of them had had a ship blown out from under him. They were a salty lot and very good at their jobs.

Presence of the ferry crew surely made life good for me. I did not have a damn thing to do but enjoy the experience. Had I been at all conscientious about my duties with the radar equipment, I would have immersed myself in learning how to work the radar and in studying manuals that were readily available. In fact, I was urged to do so by my division officer, a young Virginian, Joseph Francis Dillon. He was a nice guy, but didn't have the foggiest notion of what he was doing. Intelligent, but oh my, what a dilbert. He and I never did come to understand each other. I made no effort to do so, and he was very uncomfortable in any kind of leadership role. He was simply inept at such things. But, he was our "superior officer." Actually, his lack of savvy made life better for me in most situations. Once in a while it backfired and cost me dearly. However, during the trip down the Ohio and Mississippi he stayed out of the way. So, instead of assimilating the content of those radar manuals, I soaked up the ever changing scenery.

Radar equipment on an LST was used for navigational purposes. It was located in the chart room, immediately adjacent to a large table on which the navigation charts were always spread out. It was on those navigation charts that our position was plotted at all times. Also located on that chart table were books, Navy documents containing descriptions of our next destination, including information helpful to navigating the waters of an unfamiliar port, plus some general information about the places we were approaching. When there were no officers in the chart room, which was most of the time, I could read a bit and get some idea of what to expect at the next port of call. The stuff was by no means essential, but it was interesting. Going down the Ohio river, for example: Length of the Ohio River-981 miles—Number of locks-53—Low water is between July and November—Widest point 5,910 feet at 946 miles below Pittsburgh and 22.5 miles above the mouth of the river. This stuff added interest to the journey, pulled it together.

Pittsburgh to New Orleans via the two great rivers is downhill all the way. A vast, complex system of locks is in place to move ships through the otherwise unnavigable spots along the river. Observing the way our ship was passed in and out of those locks was an incredible experience for me. I stood at the rail watching the procedure at most every lock we passed through. The ferry crew expertly eased the ship into the locks, enormous doors of the lock closed behind us, water level inside the lock was then lowered until it matched that of the river. Then doors at the bow end of the ship would open and off we'd go downstream.

The wheelhouse was a good place to hangout at any time day or night. Ordinarily there would be three crewmen on duty, a helmsman, a quartermaster, and a man at the enunciators. The helmsman, of course, was at the wheel, steering the ship as ordered by the officer on duty in the conning tower located above the wheelhouse. To the right of the helm were the enunciators, a mechanism used to notify those in the engine room when a change in engine speed or a reversing of the engines was ordered. The quartermaster stayed busy at a stand-up desk, maintaining a log of most everything that transpired. Because the radar gear was located only a few feet away, I heard everything that was going on out in the wheelhouse. Whenever anything interesting was happening I could step through the hatchway and become a part of the event. The view from the wheelhouse was good, too. Just outside the wheelhouse was the boat deck, an even better spot for soaking up the sights. One could be attuned to whatever was happening.

While the ferry crew was in charge, the wheelhouse took on a theatrical quality. It became a center for the spinning of tall tales and astonishing exhibitions. The men in the ferry crew loved to tell sea stories. Everyone realized the stories were generously embellished, but we neophytes found them to be good entertainment and no harm done. Louie, a member of the ferry crew, revealed a tattoo the likes of which could not have been duplicated many times among the sixteen million folks in the United States military of World War II. Louie had the guts (or stupidity) to get this preposterous tattoo, as well as the audacity to display it. He put his tattoo on exhibit anytime he could attract an audience, and Louie never had a problem gathering dumbfounded witnesses. One afternoon, early in our journey down the river, Louie was on duty at the helm, and telling some interesting tales of his sex life. At the conclusion of one of his raucous stories his buddy, the quartermaster, said. "Louie, when are you gonna show these guys your pride and joy?" Louie needed no coaxing. He signaled the quartermaster to take over at the helm. The wheelhouse became Louie's stage. Louie unbuckled his belt, dropped his blue jeans, and whipped out his enormous penis. That gesture in itself would have been quite a performance, debunking the claim that all men are created equal. But the size of his penis was not the feature attraction. His real pride was the tattoo. On Louie's penis was tattooed, MY PAL...But there was more. Louie dropped his jeans and skivvies, raised his denim shirt and said, "Get a load of my snake. A lady tattoo artist did all of my tattoos. Ain't that snake somethin? See how she did the snake coming out of the crack of my ass, then around to my belly. And here's the head just about to go in my navel. I bet none of you guys ever seen no better tattoos than what I got." Louie posed long enough for all assembled in the wheelhouse to thoroughly examine and appreciate his decorations before he put his clothes back together and returned to duty at the helm. The poor guy sincerely believed that those tattoos made him a real somebody. Perhaps he was right. I certainly could not put a claim on anything that distinguished me in any way. Word of Louie's tattoos passed quickly. He became the number one attraction among the crew. Surely he would have been an attraction to the officers, but they had their "superior" status to uphold which prevented them from having a look at Louie's tattoos. Louie claimed that the tattoos made him a big hit with women. Maybe so. I was no favorite of any woman, but was not about to turn my penis into a sign board in order to attract them. But why not? Everything to win and nothing to lose. Hmm...I'll give that a little more thought. It's certainly worth pondering. My Navy education and my general education were moving along nicely. The course of study included diversity and was full of surprises. Not much of it appeared in The Blue Jackets Manual, but it was a fascinating curriculum.

Once we reached the confluence of the Ohio and Mississippi rivers, New Orleans seemed just around the bend. Passing Cairo, Illinois on our starboard side meant we had left the Ohio river and entered the Mississippi river. Merger of the two rivers was not particularly noticeable. A peninsula on the Illinois side gives the illusion of the two rivers blending together rather subtly. It appeared that way to me anyway. Perhaps everyone else in our crew knew that from their study of geography in school, but it was surprising to me. Me, floating down the Mississippi. Huckleberry Finn and Bob Shannon. Incredible.

A pleasant surprise at New Orleans was learning that we would be there for a while. Upon arrival we went into the Naval Repair Yard for the fixing of our bashed bottom and replacement of the two screws. This repair job would take much longer than was anticipated; a lucky punch for everyone aboard the 834. The other official business was ceremonial. That is, the formality of turning command of the ship over to Lieutenant R. J. Bentley. An oddity, it would seem, is that his official rank in the Navy was Lieutenant, but he was Captain in any and all affairs involving our ship. Captain Bentley was a peculiar little man who became more neurotic with each passing day, each new situation, every predicament we encountered. Our captain did not thrive on his circumstance.

Chapter Seven
The Shakedown Cruise

All too soon we were ready for the shakedown cruise. New screws were in place and the bottom was as good as new. In addition to those repairs, an intrusive landing craft had been loaded onto our main deck. The extensive open space was gone, disappeared when LCT 1415 was mounted and chained into place. LCT, Landing Craft Tank, is an ocean-going vessel one hundred sixty feet long and thirty-one feet wide. It was to ride all the way to Okinawa. Transporting items such as the LCT is precisely why the versatile LST was created.

A three tiered social structure emerged on our ship; the ruling class (commissioned officers), the bourgeoisie (the chief petty officer and the first class petty officers), and the lowest class, the proletariat.

I entered the Navy in the proletariat and remained a member of that group my entire tour of duty, a condition for which I have only myself to blame. My perceptions of the characters and characteristics of those who were my "superior" officers occurred from a position at the bottom of the social structure. Painfully adolescent, I was the victim of my own folly.

On November 23, 1944, we proceeded down the Mississippi River, through what is known as South Pass, and on into the Gulf of Mexico. Fortunately an experienced pilot did the navigation. Without him, I believe we would still be trying to find the way out of the swamp. Yes, there were navigation buoys to show the way, but many choices were there. Once we reached the open sea the pilot departed in his boat, Captain Bentley took command, and the fun began. He established a course that would take us to Panama City, Florida. We're off!

Objectives of the shakedown cruise were two-fold: to checkout the performance of every aspect of the new ship and to provide officers and crew with first hand experience in carrying out shipboard duties. For the ship and its inhabitants it was a time to undergo rigorous performance tests. It was, of necessity, a challenging endeavor. Everything was a clumsy, awkward undertaking. Only a small percentage of our crew, perhaps 10%, had served on other ships. For most of the ship's company, both officers and crew, this was our maiden voyage. Everything was new. We were, so to speak, at sea at sea.

For two weeks we stumbled and fumbled our way through the execution of most every function an LST could perform. Gunnery practice, beaching exercises, mock invasions, navigating and maintaining our position in a line of ships, operating the enormous bow doors, lowering the ramp onto the beach, using the stern anchor to pull the 834 off the beach, mooring alongside another ship. We acquired some much-needed familiarity with virtually every aspect of making the ship function and we learned a little seamanship. The shakedown cruise was the first time I and my radar colleague Phillip Straus got to operate the radar equipment on our own. For the two of us the shakedown was a proper shake up. It was a wake up, an initiation.

For the men learning to function as coxswains of the two power boats, the LCVPs (Landing Craft Vehicle and Personnel), the shakedown cruise was full of excitement. They were like kids. The two small boats were their toys. They played with them like children playing at war. Serious, grim, macho expressions, they thrilled to the entire process. Mornings, afternoons, and evenings of every day they practiced lowering the boats into the water, revving up the engines, racing off to the beach, dropping the bow ramp. Then reversing the entire exercise. Serious fun.

Trial and error, then trial and success. Our ignorance was visible and sometimes hazardous, but one amusing incident stands out. It involved a miscommunication between the skipper and the helmsman. Blame for the incident rested squarely on the skipper's shoulders. He was feeling his oats, his saltiness, and, in the process, came very close to running the 834 into another ship.

It was a beautiful morning. Clear skies, calm sea. The Gulf of Mexico was as quiet and pretty as a pond in Indiana. Captain Bentley was in the conning tower directing things. He was conducting some rather routine exercises, practicing changes in course and speed, putting the ship through a variety of configurations. The helmsman on duty was unfamiliar with the jargon and terminology commonly used by veteran sea captains when they communicate with the helmsman. Voice commands from the conning tower to the wheelhouse or the radarman or the radioman were transmitted through a brass tube. Upon hearing a command the helmsman was to notify the captain that he had heard and executed the command by repeating it; by answering with the same words. On this occasion, however, the helmsman became confused, befuddled. He said nothing in response to the captain's commands from the conning tower. The messages evolved into a one way communication. It went like this:

Skipper to helmsman, "Right fifteen degrees. Settle on course 090."

Helmsman to skipper: "Right fifteen degrees to course 090 Sir."

A few seconds pass in silence. Then, the Skipper in calm, rather casual tone of voice issues this command to helmsman: "Meet 'er!" There is no response from the helmsman. Dead silence in the wheelhouse. A few more seconds pass. Then, Skipper to helmsman; this time the voice reveals agitation: "Meet 'er!" Again, not a sound from the helmsman. Only a confused look, a shrug of the shoulders which said he did not understand what he was supposed to do.

A moment later the Skipper, his voice now revealing his panic, shouts: "God damn it, Meet'er!" Still nothing from the helmsman. No help from others in the wheelhouse as to what he should do. The poor perplexed follow just stood there at the wheel doing nothing. All the while the ship continued turning to starboard. The quartermaster merely motioned with his palms up, indicating that he too was dumbfounded. By this time the ship had turned well past 090 and was still turning. Skipper shouts: "Left full rudder! Reverse port engine? Starboard engine ahead full! Those commands were immediately acknowledged and relayed to the engine room. Both engines groan into the radical changes the captain commanded. Thirty seconds later, Skipper to wheelhouse, "Stop engines." A few seconds pass. Skipper to helmsman, his voice dripping with sarcasm and anger. "Now, you at the helm, you are coming up on 090. Can you see that?"

Helmsman: "Yes Captain."

Skipper says: "Then slowly adjust the wheel so our turn to port slows. Ease the rudder, ease the turn so that when we get to 090 you have met that bearing smoothly and we can proceed on course 090. Engines ahead one third.

Helmsman: "Aye, Captain. Ahead one third. Steady on course 090."

A moment later the captain entered the wheelhouse, having made his way down the two ladders that led from the conning tower to the signal deck and on down to the boat deck where the wheelhouse was located. He was livid. Furious. He raged at the helmsman: "What in the hell are you doing at the wheel? Why didn't you follow my commands? Can't you hear? I ought to put you in the brig. I ought to have you court-martialed. You damn near ran us into another ship. How do you think this makes me look? You've made me the laughing stock of every officer in this training group. And they'll be talking about it. Word gets back. My record is perfect and I want it to stay that way. Why did you ignore my clear and repeated command to MEET'ER? Why?"

The intimidated kid at the helm meekly replied, "I don't know what you mean when you tell me to meet 'er."

Exasperated, the skipper said, "It means just that. Meet 'er. Plain and simple, meet 'er. That's all. It means, with the wheel, that thing you're holding with both hands, ease the rudder back so when the ship gets turned to the new course you settle gently and smoothly on that course and on she goes. Nothing complicated. It's real simple."

From the wheelhouse Captain Bentley spoke through the tube to the officer of the day in the conning tower, directing him to proceed to our anchorage, drop anchor, and secure for the day. Bentley then came through the navigation room, passed behind me, went down the ladder and into his private domain, his captain's suite. A nasty incident had passed and everyone survived. The skipper's tirade no doubt happened because he was frightened and embarrassed. It did not take long for all of the helmsmen to get the word on the command, "Meet'er." And everyone aboard the 834 learned a little more about the kind of man we had as our captain.

That incident notwithstanding, the shakedown cruise was a success. All of the objectives were accomplished. An official stamp of approval was given on December 7, 1944 when a party of officers came aboard and conducted a perfunctory, ritual-like inspection of ship and crew. It was labeled the Annual Military Inspection of USS LST 834. The inspection party decreed that we had earned a good record for the shakedown cruise and extended their wish for good sailing, a safe journey, and successful engagement of the enemy.

Late that same day we arrived at Gulfport, Mississippi. There was no special mention of the significance of the date or how the events of December 7, 1941, the Japanese attack on Pearl Harbor, had put us on LST 834. Nothing. Bow doors were opened, the ramp lowered, and the tank deck took on a load of wood pilings. A weird cargo. Presumably the pilings were part of the grand plan for winning the war. Our first contribution to defeating the Japanese was to haul a bunch of logs to some place where there were no trees big enough to be used for whatever purpose our cargo was intended. One wonders. Ammunition, food, and fuel supplies were replenished. Army troops bound for Panama came aboard. Our cargo was complete.

A few problems with mechanical operations of the ship were discovered on the shakedown. Nothing major, but putting things completely ship-shape was considered prudent. Consequently, we returned to New Orleans and a brief reprieve. A few more liberties in New Orleans while repairs were made at the navy yard were welcomed, of course. But, much to my surprise, there came a special bonus; a seventy-two hour pass. I chose to hop on the train and go all the way to Indiana. What a stupid idea that was. I was in Fort Wayne for twelve of the seventy-two hours. Sixty hours traveling on a half dozen trains. What made it even more regrettable is that I met a gorgeous red head at the train station in Montgomery, Alabama. The train had been delayed in Montgomery. Outside the train station there was a hospitality cart where some women were dispensing coffee and doughnuts to military personnel passing through Montgomery. A lovely girl was in charge of the doughnuts. We chatted for twenty minutes or so. When the conductor called out the "All aboard," she urged me to change my plans and let her show me Montgomery. Fool that I was, I boarded the train. I wasted the

entire seventy-two hours and squandered what might have been the

opportunity of a lifetime.

Chapter Eight
Panama

December 19, 1944, we left New Orleans, bound for the Panama Canal. Weather was perfect. Water in the Gulf of Mexico was a magnificent blue. The entire setting was peaceful. I was totally oblivious to the war. But while I was in what was a downright pleasurable situation, final plans for the invasion of Okinawa were cooking.

At a November meeting of Admiral Nimitz, Admiral King, General Buckner, Vice Admiral Turner and some lesser figures, Buckner and Turner disagreed on certain aspects of the plan. Buckner did not like the March 1 landing date. His contention was that March 1 was too early because weather conditions at that time could mean still northeast winds that would cause the surf to be too high to beach landing craft. In December, after considerable study and discussion, the landing date was changed form March 1 to April 1, a decision that no doubt saved the lives of thousands of Americans in every branch of the military. Amphibious craft of all kinds were to be central to the planned invasion of Okinawa. Heavy seas would certainly swamp smaller landing craft loaded with troops and equipment. Insisting on the April 1, 1945 date proved to be a powerful prescience of the part of General Buckner.

Occurrence of the unexpected soon became the norm on the 834. The mix of personalities and talents (or lack thereof) seemed to establish incongruous situations that were often very funny. One took place in my berthing compartment midway through the first morning of our journey across the Gulf of Mexico. The compartment was not really mine, of course. It contained fifteen bunks and fifteen lockers for the fifteen men who lived there. At one end of it there was a hatch that led to a storage compartment below. The lid to that hatch was about three feet square and raised about six inches above the deck, making a surface that could double as a table if you sat on the deck. On that particular morning, the first day out of New Orleans en route to Panama, two machinist mates chose to make the hatch a table where they could have a little beer party. That decision is what set up the circumstance for an incident that was sad, funny, and unforgettable. Three characters were involved; Koch, Holes, and Lichek. Tony Danapas played a minor role of sycophant to Lichek. Koch and Holes were from Hoboken, New Jersey. Their on-duty hours were spent below decks in the engine room where noise of the engines was maddening. It was a horrible place to spend four minutes, let alone a full four hour watch. But Koch and Holes stayed in good spirits. They were funny, unassuming guys who took nothing too seriously. When they were not on duty they were in their bunks. Both spoke Hobokenese with a strong Joisey accent. They were the perfect Mutt and Jeff team. Koch was a tall fellow, Holes was a little guy. Each one wore a mustache. They always had the soggy remains of a cigar in their mouths. Two marvelous guys. But along came Lichek.

Ensign Lichek was the commissioned officer in charge of the First Division. Deck hands, shipfitters boatswains, and coxswains were all in the First Division. Lichek's job was to see that the 834 stayed clean and neat, rust free and painted. He was Mr. Ship-shape. A tall, thin fellow, I never saw him when he was not wearing dark sunglasses. I don't know if the sunglasses were part of an image he sought to project or if he had some unusual sensitivity to light. Ensign Lichek was perfect for the cast of the Gilbert and Sullivan opera, H.M.S. Pinafore. He was the real life version of the character who sang, "I cleaned the windows and swept the floor, and I polished up the handle of the big front door, I polished up the handle so carefully that now I am the ruler of the queen's Navy, I thought so little they rewarded me by making me the ruler of the queen's navy." Lichek was the only regular Navy man among our commissioned officers. The Navy was his life. World War II enabled him to raise his status to heights beyond his wildest pre-war Navy dreams. He jumped from being a non-commissioned petty officer to a commission as an ensign. The man was well suited for his task as leader of the deck hands. It was his level of competence. What seemed to be his most cherished, most gratifying mission was inspecting the living quarters of the crew. That is what he was doing when he burst in on Koch and Holes in the midst of their beer party.

It was mid-morning of the first day out of New Orleans en route to Panama. I was at my locker. Koch and Holes were seated nearby, laughing, enjoying their beer. Setting on the deck in front of them were six or eight bottles of beer they had brought on board when they returned to the ship after a final liberty in New Orleans the night before. Both men were having a grand time. In the blink of an eye their conviviality turned to despair. Ensign Lichek, on one his impromptu inspections the crew soon learned to dread, stepped into the compartment. Party's over. Lichek was ecstatic. He had won a round of his favorite game, "Gotcha." His inspection had hit pay dirt. He had found two men guilty of violating ship's regulations on our very first day at sea. Tony Danapas was, as always, trailing along immediately behind Lichek. Lichek spoke. "Danapas, accompany these two men and their beer topside and watch them dump it into the sea. See to it at once." Lichek left the scene at once. Koch and Holes were, of course, devastated. All of their beer went to the bottom of the Gulf of Mexico. Both men were put on report.

Subsequently they received a dose of extra duty as punishment for their crime. It was a memorable introduction to the style of Ensign Lichek.

As the months passed by, I too was to experience the wrath of Ensign Lichek. For some reason he took special pleasure in nailing me for extra duty, finding some satisfaction in watching me work. The man didn't smile much, at least not around me. His expression was more of a sneer or a smirk, a look that said, "I've got you now you son-of-a-bitch." I remember one situation in particular that happened after we had been out in the Pacific for some months. We were anchored at Funa Futi, a tiny island near the equator. As usual, I was working off extra duty. On this occasion I was over the side, standing on a platform suspended by ropes, painting the side of the ship. The water was very calm. Even so, because of the bathtub shape of an LST, it always has some roll to it. My platform was just above the water line. With each roll of the ship I was dipped up to my crotch into the water. Back and forth, back and forth, into the water, then out, over and over and over. It was kind of refreshing, actually. I happened to glance up, and there he was, brother Lichek, leaning on the rail, gazing down at me, enjoying my plight, with that weird look of satisfaction on his face. A peculiar old bird was Lichek.

The other officers were less enamored with their status. None of them were regular Navy. Most had not finished college when they were brought into the military. They were green as grass ensigns, but made no pretense to hide their inexperience. Charles Latz was the most personable, most affable of the young officers, and he turned out to be the most competent as well. My division officer, Joseph Francis Dillon, was a Virginia boy. He knew very little about the various specializations of the men under his command, but that was not his fault. He had been arbitrarily assigned to command the communications division on the 834. That was it. Dillon seemed to be an intelligent fellow, but boy what a Dilbert of a guy. A smart fellow, but out of his field. Certainly not as far out of his field as me. I had no field. Dillon must have spent many an hour pondering how he could get me going in the right direction, become more of an asset to the operation. The man was a tolerant, harmless person most of the time. I was fortunate to have had him as my division officer. It was almost as though I had no division officer. That was fortunate, indeed.

Other than the aborted beer party, nothing untoward happened during the six day voyage to Panama. All things considered, it was a very pleasant journey.

Chapter Nine
Christmas Among the Cuties of Colón

On Christmas day we anchored at the Caribbean end of the Panama Canal, Coco Solo Naval Operating Base, Panama. The army troops disembarked immediately. They were happy to get off the 834 and we were happy to see them go. Transporting troops was a basic function of the 834, but it was a role almost everyone accepted begrudgingly. Troops aboard meant a bunch of strangers moving in, sharing your bathroom, eating your food, getting in the way, making a mess, and finally departing without so much as a thank you. Thank yous were certainly not on anyone's mind when we got to Okinawa and troops were heading ashore to an uncertain fate. But the troops getting off at Panama were anxious to do so because fate had dealt them the good fortune of missing a trip to the war in the Pacific. Comparatively, Panama was a cushy duty. Overseas pay at a place as far distant from combat as you could get. Those men were handed a double bonus in the form of Colón, the city located at the Caribbean entrance to the Panama Canal. It contained everything a G. I. looked for in a liberty town. Minimum essentials were booze and brothels. If a town offered anything more it was happily received, but not considered necessary for a satisfying outing on the town. Colón passed the test most emphatically. A bar on every corner and a few more in between. Most of the saloons were run down, disreputable joints. All of them were filled with U.S. Military personnel. It was an ideal situation for everyone concerned.

The whores of Colón were everywhere. Hundreds were headquartered in a mangy old hotel. The girls partitioned their "private" spaces with curtains. Along the street the more expensive ladies languished in doorways where they posed in what they perceived to be a most alluring costume. As I passed by the door of one particularly enticing maiden she asked, "Hey kid, how about a little of that French stuff?" That was difficult to pass up, but I was a bit scared to give it a go. Maybe she was really French, the grandchild of a lady left behind in 1889 when France gave up on their attempt to build the canal. Who knows? But the brothels of Colón were not limited to French girls. It was truly an international operation. Take your pick; fat, skinny, tall, short, old, young, black, white, pink…the U.S. Navy kept them all in business. Liberty in Colón was certainly a novel way to spend Christmas Eve. It brought new meaning to "Merry Christmas to all and to all a good night."

Another Christmas gift was peculiar in a different way. Every man received a Red Cross package containing a woolen sweater, a woolen hat, a woolen scarf, a pair of woolen gloves; all the items in Navy blue, of course. Ladies all across America had hand knit each item. Marvelous intentions, however, Panama was boiling hot and we were headed for the South Pacific. We had no use for the lovingly crafted merchandise and no place to store it. It was a dilemma.

December 27, 1944 we passed through the Panama Canal. Me, going through the Panama Canal! Unbelievable. This was a real adventure. Into the lock, the ship raised up to Lake Gatun, crossing the lake with no noise, no congestion, no sign of war. Amazing. The twenty-four mile cruise across Lake Gatun was beautiful. Then the drop down to the Pacific via thirty-one feet to Lake Cross, on to Miraflores Lock, then down another fifty-four feet to sea level and the final eight mile channel to the Pacific Ocean. A spectacular experience, indeed.

Chapter Ten
Amos

In convoy with two other LSTs we sailed west, then northwest. Our destination, San Diego, California. At sundown I turned on the radar, assuming the first watch of the night. I expected it to be a routine four hour watch at the radar, but it didn't work out that way. I remained at the radar the entire night. My colleague, Amos Straus, was scheduled to relieve me at midnight, however, this was the night I was to learn about his sleeping habits. Sometimes it was impossible to waken him once he fell asleep. This night was one of those times. A few minutes before midnight I notified the officer on watch in the conning tower that I would be away from the radar long enough to waken my relief. I went below to our living quarters and found Amos in a deep sleep. I took hold of his enormous forearm, gave it a good shake, and called his name. I didn't call out loudly because there were fourteen other shipmates snoring comfortably. I shook Amos again and again to no avail. No reaction from my comrade. I gave him another aggressive tug and Amos lashed out, throwing his mighty fist in the general direction of my head. I managed to dodge out of the way. I shook him again. This time the fist brushed my jaw, but he was still sleeping soundly. Enough of that. I gave up, returned to the radar and stayed on watch until dawn. Ten hours. Once there was daylight I shut down the radar, went below, and crawled into my bunk. Amos slept on. This was the first of many occasions when I was at the radar all night. But it was okay. The trade-offs with Amos were very much in my favor. Whenever his solid sleeping resulted in my doing an all night watch he would waken, well rested but genuinely repentant, always begging me to be more strident in my effort to waken him.

Amos was one of the finest persons I have ever known. We were the same age. Other than that, we were as different as two people could possibly be. Nonetheless, Amos became a trusted, loyal, dependable friend and colleague. He would do anything for me. A strong, powerful fellow, he frequently stepped in and saved me from getting my teeth knocked down my throat while we were on liberty in some strange port or even aboard ship. Often he would say to me, "Come on, let's trade blows." I would double up my fist and hit him in the stomach as hard as I could swing. He never flinched. His abdominal muscles were rock hard. For his half of the challenge he would retaliate by giving me a mild punch in the belly and my flimsy frame would collapse from the blow.

Amos had a sense of responsibility that set him aside from everyone else. In boot camp, for example, he established himself as something special in an amusing way. The incident was not an attempt to be conspicuously better than the rest. It was simply the way he went about every incident that came along. That is, he took on a task and gave it his best, whatever the circumstance. We were in different companies in boot camp, but were assigned to the same dining hall for a week of mess duty. One day he and I were assigned to clean the oven. It was, I believe, the biggest oven of all time, big enough to accommodate Phillip Straus on the inside. Amos attacked that oven as no one had ever done before. He literally crawled inside the oven and gave it a thorough cleaning. I served as his gofer, bringing fresh cloths and fresh water and some special brush he needed. When he crawled out of that oven he was black and greasy from head to toe, but that damned oven was immaculate. The chief cook in that mess hall also watched Amos crawl from the oven. He was flabbergasted at the sight, but was singing the praises of Amos all over the place. In but one day Amos established himself as a fabled hero of the mess halls. That same determination, his sense

Edwin Straus, my radar colleague

of responsibility, was with him wherever we went, whatever the task. He taught himself to be a radar technician by studying the repair and maintenance manuals diligently and applying what he learned to fine tuning our radar equipment. No one required him to do so. It was simply an intellectual curiosity, a compulsion to do things thoroughly and properly. He could diagnose and repair any malfunctions that occurred with our radar equipment.

A foolish fellow was supposed to handle the radar repair and maintenance tasks, but he was a fraud and a liar. Pappy Partin was his name. The guy was a worthless character who successfully bamboozled our division officer for a long time. On one occasion Partin lied about a situation involving me in order to make himself look like the white knight. He succeeded. I did not learn of his deceit until a year later, long after the damage was done. That was life on the 834. It was a setting in which everyone lived the motto, "Trust everyone, but watch 'em."

Somehow Amos learned how to shoot craps. I have no idea where and how he picked that up, but he surely knew how to toss the dice. Whenever we tied up alongside another LST for the night

Amos would step across to the other ship, become involved in a crap game, and come back with their money. Smart! Yes, indeed. But much more than being intellectually smart, he was street smart as well. Amos possessed all of the attributes one could desire in a friend and a colleague. I believe he could have succeeded in any academic discipline. He would have been a great college athlete, too. But he chose to go back home to Galesburg, Illinois, took a job in the brickyard, and that was it. I am sure he was a great asset to the brickyard, but he had the potential to excel in any profession. A phenomenal individual who looked out for me all the way from Pittsburgh to Okinawa to China, that was Amos.

Why is it that some guys get pinned with some absurd nickname, wherever they happen to be? With Edwin Straus it was Amos. And me? Bob Malin, a Coxswain from Ohio, decided I resembled a comic strip character named Snuffy Smith. Snuffy Smith was a pitiful looking guy who was always in trouble, always messing up some way. One day I was sitting on an ammunition box and Bob Malin walked by. He hesitated, then turned back to me and said, "I've got it! Snuffy Smith! You remind me of Snuffy Smith, the guy in the comics." Unfortunately, it stuck. Snuffy became my moniker.

It certainly was no compliment, but it stuck. Snuffy. Holy Jesus,

what a name.

Snuffy Smith

Snuffy Shannon

Bob Malin decided I resembled the character in Laswell's comic

strip so I became Snuffy for the duration.

Chapter Eleven
Clap, Crabs, Infections and Inspections

Memories were not all that we carried with us when we sailed

away from the Panama Canal Zone. Within three days the passageway

outside sick bay was lined with shipmates suffering from dripping

penises, itching crotches, and infected bodies. Clap (Gonorrhea)

and Crabs (pubic lice) were going away presents from the lovely

ladies in the brothels of Colón. Minor infections were acquired in

the tattoo parlors. More cases emerged in the next few days. All the

instructions and admonitions we had received were for naught. Eros

the mischief-maker had taken over.

Penicillin took care of the Gonorrhea in but a few days. Getting rid of the crab infestations was more complicated. Those pesky creatures refused to surrender. They hung on, requiring much scrubbing of bodies, clothing and bedding. The fellows with crabs were miserable with the itching and scratching and sleeplessness and nervousness. Those who were not suffering with the crabs found the sufferers good targets for teasing, which, of course, only compounded the misery for the pubic lice carriers. Those tiny little bugs attached themselves to the crotch much the same way as a crab in the sea attaches itself to something and refuses to let go. They dug in and hung on. Hot weather and cramped living conditions and miserable daily lives of the victims were made to order for the lice.

The near epidemic of Clap and crabs prompted a short arm inspection for all hands. On this occasion the main deck was the short arm inspection center. Each man drops his drawers for the pharmacist mate who says, "Skin'er back and milk'er down...Okay, now turn around...Bend over and spread your cheeks...Next." Following the short arm inspection the pharmacist mate spoke briefly to the assembled crew, urging us to come for treatment, assuring us that no one would be punished for contracting a venereal disease. Ensign Lichek promptly negated what the pharmacist mate had said by growling, "Anyone who gets the clap gets the brig if I find out about it." Lichek was a throwback to Victorian times. He and Captain Bligh would have made a great team.

Once minor infections cleared up, tattoos acquired in Panama were put on display. A good many of my shipmates had visited tattoo parlors. Now they proudly showed off their new decorations. It is amazing how those tattoos added swagger and self-esteem. Some sort of a badge, like a membership in an exclusive club. For a good many men in the Navy of world War II a tattoo contributed to their image of themselves as salty, genuine sailors, men of the world, machismo. One pitiful soul went shirtless as much as possible because he loved to display the tattoos above each breast...Sweet and Sour.

Eight or nine days out of Panama I was sitting on that ammunition box topside again, idly looking out at the sea, chatting with one of the cooks. Pete Ruskin, one of the deck hands, joined us. Pete was a strong, handsome, curly headed blond, a fun-loving guy who laughed easily, and seemed not a to have a care in the world. He was delighted with the tattoo on his forearm that he had acquired in Panama. It was two hearts intertwined, with Norma and Pete inscribed across the hearts. I asked him why he got the tattoo. "Norma, she's my girl," Pete answered. "Every time I look at this tattoo I think of my Norma, back home waiting for me. We're gonna get married as soon as the war is over. My beautiful Norma." When the mail caught up with us in San Diego, Pete's letter from his "beautiful Norma" contained some shocking news. But on this day he was in great spirits.

The cook then told me about the tattoo he would get when we arrived in San Diego. "It's gonna be a tribute to my mom. It's gonna be a rose, right here on my upper arm, and below it it's gonna say, Mother." I thought the guy was kidding. I laughed. Another mistake on my part. He damn near threw me over the side. That was the last time I got involved in a discussion of tattoos. To sailors of that era a tattoo was kind of like a religious symbol. Better just keep quiet about it.

Weather remained good and seas moderate throughout the twelve day journey to San Diego. We acquired a good deal of badly needed knowledge of what it is like to function as a team in making a shipboard society work. Savvy. That's what we were acquiring. Accumulating savvy is tough going. On a ship like ours the process required a whole lot of give and take. Not everyone was compatible with the give portion of that philosophy. The peculiarities and idiosyncrasies of each person become so visible and, in certain cases, they are nearly impossible to endure. The different ways people eat, for example. What is considered normal to one man sitting at a mess table is considered crude and rude to the person sitting beside him. One must adapt to the scene without comment. That's it! Adapt. One of the radiomen would go for several days without a shower or a change of clothing, including a change of socks. His bunk was near mine. Boy, did he stink. The guy was oblivious to his own odor. I never reached the point where I was oblivious to his stinking body, but accepted the fact that there was not a damn thing I could do about it.

For Amos and me the twelve days at sea sailing in convoy gave us plenty of experience in using radar to maintain the position of the 834 in relation to the other ships in the convoy. It was invaluable training for us because the ships altered position frequently; sometimes in the lead, sometimes in the middle, sometimes trailing. We began to feel comfortable with our responsibility. That new-found expertise paid off unexpectedly when we neared San Diego. After having enjoyed perfect weather conditions throughout the journey, we encountered a heavy fog when we reached San Diego Bay on January 8, 1945. Radar demonstrated its unique capability of being able to see through the fog and show the way into the bay. Thanks to Amos we arrived without mishap.

Chapter Twelve
Dear John

First man ashore in San Diego was the mailman, off to the base post office with a bag full of letters home. Spirits soared when he returned to the ship with our first mail call since New Orleans. Letters and packages had caught up with us at last. For some fellows this was a great moment. For others it was doubly demoralizing. Not to get any mail after such a long time really tore a guy apart. To watch other men receive a fistful of letters and escape to the pleasures those letters brought was more than one could take. Mail call meant a warm embrace from family, friends and sweetheart in the form of letters, photographs, and packages. To be left out entirely was devastating. But it happened. Disappointed, crestfallen, it was an awkward moment for those who had gotten mail and for those who had not. Sharing letters became a common practice to buck up the spirits of those who got nothing, but that idea only compounded a fellow's misery.

Some who received mail wished they had not. Those men were torn apart when they read the letter from one they loved. It was the beginning of heartache time on the 834. The very first mail call delivered "Dear John" letters, letters from loved ones who know longer loved...sweethearts back home had found somebody new. Regardless of the sweetheart's skill in letting the guy down softly, the message was ultimately the same...A blunt notification that a wife was divorcing her husband or a sweetheart was breaking off a romance. Each of those letters was a reminder that absence makes the heart grow fonder for somebody else. When a "Dear John" was found among his letters the poor fellow would, of course, become terribly despondent. Condolences from shipmates fell on deaf ears. The heartbroken guy who had been cast aside by his love wandered around in a daze, disbelieving this could happen. Some fellows became bitter and short tempered, needing to take their grief and frustration out on somebody or something.

Meanwhile, other shipmates rejoiced with their lipstick decorated love letters that declared and assured never-ending love. Sympathetic to the suffering souls who received the "Dear John" they proclaimed to all that such a fate would never be theirs. "That's never going to happen to me. She's just not that way." Next mail call would invariably be his turn to get the "Dear John".

Pete Ruskin got his turn with that first batch of mail at San Diego. The indelible pigment that scarred his arm with the Norma tattoo was hardly dry when he received news that Norma had found a new sweetheart. For the rest of his life he could look at the Norma on his arm, but never again would he see the Norma that he loved. Pete was both broken hearted and embarrassed. He swore that he was going to jump ship, go absent without leave back to Hobart, Indiana and destroy the guy who had stolen his Norma. Perhaps the threat was only a face-saving gesture. Wisely, Pete did not jump ship. Pete was certainly not alone. Only a very few of my shipmates escaped the dreaded "Dear John." My status as a guy without a sweetheart had at least one compensating element: I would never receive the "Dear John."

Using a sailor's criteria for evaluating the qualities of a town, San Diego, in 1945, got high marks. It was a fine little city on the sea. Historically a Navy town, wartime made the Navy base central to the goings on in San Diego. The boys of the 834 had fully recovered from Panama's damsel delivered diseases and they were ready to go. It was liberty time in a new port, a time to taste the delights of its booze and brothels.

Pete Ruskin
Wonderful fellow who wore "Norma" tattoo long after he lost
Norma

A daytime mission in downtown San Diego had some negative repercussions on my already faltering Navy career. Pappy Partin and I were sent into town to pick up some spare parts for the radar equipment. Partin was nick-named Pappy because he looked and acted like an old man. He might have been thirty-five. The guy was worthless, but he knew how to manipulate a person or a situation to his own benefit. Ultimately he figured out how to get off the ship and be sent home. A real conniver, he was. But I didn't know that on the day we went into San Diego together, which was too bad for me.

We picked up a small box of spare parts and found ourselves with nothing to do. Plenty of time for mischief. Partin suggested that we stop somewhere for a beer. It was not yet noon, too early for beer for me, but just right for Partin. I left him at a bar, telling him I would return in a couple hours. That plan seemed to fit in just right with what he had in mind. Sure enough, when I returned he was in heaven; draped over some God-awful woman in the corner of the bar. I took the box of spare parts and told Partin I was going on back to the ship. That did it. He quickly finished his beer, made arrangements to meet the lady in the evening, and we caught a bus back to the Navy base.

When we arrived at the ship Partin took the box of parts and told me he would deliver them to Ensign Dillon. That was fine with me. I did not expect him use the situation to make himself look clean as a whistle while inferring that I had run off to mess around. That was a bad misjudgment on my part. It was many months later that I learned that Partin had deliberately lied to Dillon about the little San Diego excursion. He concocted a tale about how I had disappeared and he spent the whole day trying to track me down. Dillon believed him. Partin was promoted to petty officer shortly thereafter. I remained a seaman. So it goes. Partin's shenanigans got worse. Finally, at Guadalcanal, just before we headed for the invasion of Okinawa, Partin was caught in a web of his own making, a situation that did him in for good. But the guy was an excellent liar. His downfall did not occur until after the 834 had logged a few thousand nautical miles across the Pacific Ocean.

Chapter Thirteen
To Hawaii

Can this actually be happening to me? That question kept recurring. Despite the situation I was in and the highly unfavorable prospects for my immediate future, I was fired up, excited. I was on my way to Hawaii. I was a minor player aboard an uninspiring ship, which was transporting a dreary cargo. Nonetheless, I was headed for an exotic tropical island. The war was still a long way off, the venture still fun and games.

Before leaving San Diego we had taken on 15,000 gallons of fuel oil, 286 bags of mail, and two new officers. The two officers were excess baggage assigned to the 834 from a surplus officers pool.

Their responsibilities had to be invented. Both of them soon made decisions that turned me against them for keeps.

Letters we wrote were censored, a practice that commenced as soon as we left the United States. Presumably, the censoring was to make sure we did not send any messages that could be useful to the Japanese. None of us knew anything that could have been of value to the Japanese. Nevertheless, our letters were all carefully read by the guy designated as censor, in this case Ensign Brown, one of the two new officers. Lacking anything else to do, and delighted to play the role, Brown allowed himself to get carried away with his new responsibility, expanding the scope of his task to include making judgments on the morality of our letters. He screened letters carefully, sorting out words or obscenities he found objectionable. One of my high school chums was with the infantry fighting in Germany. We corresponded now and then. Ensign Brown found one of my letters to Tom a bit heavy with obscenities. He returned the letter, saying "I cannot allow your letter to leave the ship because of the language you have used." Superior officer Brown's eyes beheld sin of some sort in my letter. Useful to the Japanese? Hardly. I had violated his sin list. He had violated my first amendment rights. In his view first amendment rights had been shelved for the duration of the war, or at least for the duration of my time as his subordinate. Maybe the guy was a preacher. When Brown confronted me with the letter I tossed it into the sea. My friend never got the opportunity to enjoy my obscene message.

The convoy for our ten day voyage to Hawaii consisted of three LSTs and a minesweeper. Weather conditions were ideal, with balmy days and nights. Radar revealed our position in the convoy. My responsibility was to keep the officer in the conning tower posted on any significant changes in our position. Occasionally the helmsman would fail to pay attention to what he was doing and we would stray off course. I could detect this immediately on the radar and report it to the officer on duty. It was simply a matter of staying focused on the radar screen, just as the helmsman needed to keep his focus on the compass. But staying focused was difficult for everyone after a few days at sea. The tasks were so monotonous, so repetitious, that a kind of listlessness, a boredom, was inevitable. Any kind of interruption or variation in the routines served as a welcome break. Anything for a laugh or a new topic for conversation was welcome. Often it got a bit silly, a little slaphappy. The helmsman might spontaneously break into song. Regardless of the quality of his singing or the selection of his song, it was good to hear. One little ditty went like this:

Christopher Columbo.

Thought the world was roundo,

That navigatin', masturbatin',

Son-of-a-bitch, Columbo.

That was it, the entire song, but it always made me laugh. Perhaps it was the setting, the incongruity of it all. Even the Skipper's peculiarities became welcome diversions.

Radar and the navigation table

Watching him smoke a cigarette was a fascinating sideshow. The captain was a night owl. At some time during the night he would suddenly appear: no special time, no schedule... it was impossible to predict when he would show up. Captain Bentley would appear in the navigation room and immediately light up a cigarette. Blackout regulations prohibited smoking anywhere topside at night. Because of that prohibition the captain spent a lot of time in the navigation room pondering our position as it had been plotted on the charts. Cigarette smoking always accompanied his ponderings. My position at the radar was no more than three feet from where the captain would stand as he examined the charts and smoked. I became a student of his unique smoking style.

Captain Bentley literally consumed smoke. Not only did he ingest the smoke, he digested it as well. Watching him inhale the first drag was a sight to behold. I believe he ingested fully half of a cigarette with his first long, lingering, drawn-out drag. That initial drag must have circulated smoke into every cavity in his body. As he drew on the cigarette, sucking smoke deeper and deeper into his lungs, his eyes began to bulge out of his head; looking as though they were certain to pop out of their sockets. For a long, long period of time after ingesting the smoke, none of it would re-emerge. It was as though he had eaten the smoke; swallowed it, digested it just as one would do with food. After a seemingly interminable amount of time had passed, the smoke would begin to seep back out of his body, flowing out through his nostrils and mouth. Maybe the smoke leaked from his ears, too. He did not blow the smoke out. No, he merely allowed it to flow from his innards. When his body had emptied of smoke he repeated the process…very deliberately. His smoking ritual never varied, never ceased. The only good thing about his incessant smoking is that it provided something for me to watch. It was an awesome demonstration, indeed.

Two of my many crude habits quite understandably irritated Captain Bentley. Watching someone chew gum is, in itself, sufficient cause for irritation. But what made the gum chewing absolutely disgusting was a crass habit of cracking it. One night, when I was at the radar and Captain Bentley was beside me at the navigation table, he blew a gasket. He shouted, "Shannon, if you crack that gum once more I'm going to throw you in the brig for keeps." I dropped my gum into the waste basket. Bentley, eyeing me with complete disdain, took another drag on his cigarette. No more chewing gum for me. But the cigarette smoking continued undiminished.

A rather cruel way of relieving boredom at sea was to make fun of some vulnerable shipmate. There were plenty of vulnerable guys on the 834. One fellow, Larry Herendeen, was subjected to so much personal harassment that he began to behave in a very peculiar way, and his peculiar way made him a more enticing guy to harass. Larry was a high strung, fidgety guy from Boston. He was one of those guys whose speech pattern skipped the r in every word. Pahk ya cah, for park your car, for example. Shipmates gave him a lot of attention because of the way he talked; often mimicking him. I believe he liked that. He came to exaggerate his idiosyncratic pronunciations and enunciations just because he enjoyed the attention. But another mannerism Larry nurtured in order to get attention almost drove him crazy.

Mess compartments doubled as gathering places for the crew when not on duty. They were convenient spots for letter writing and chatting. Men would sit at tables on either side of the passageway.

Now and then a man passing through would get goosed: that is, he got someone's finger up his ass. Every man in the crew got an occasional goose. For me, the best way to react was not to react at all. That is, don't get jumpy. A most effective response to being goosed was to stop and say to the man with his finger up your ass, "Oh, that feels good. I'll give you two hours to stop. Ooo, that's wonderful." That, of course, deflates the gooser rather than the goosee. But Larry Herendeen did just the opposite: he jumped and yelled and twisted about to avoid the goosing, establishing himself as a favorite target for tormenting. Once he had done that, the taunting became relentless. "Here he comes, guys. Goosey Larry is coming. Come on Larry, we won't get you this time. Look out behind you, Larry. No, the other side, Larry." Larry would move through the compartment with one hand on his crotch, the other hand covering his ass, a frantic expression on his face, begging and pleading to be left alone. The poor guy became an emotional wreck, but he made a fine contribution to relieving the habitual boredom of life at sea.

There was no shortage of things to complain about on the 834. Monotony, confinement, lack of privacy, no women, terrible food, a subordinate position in the pecking order, cramped quarters, bunking opposite a guy with terrible habits…the list is endless. A protective facade was worn by most everyone. With many the facade was macho. With others it was a carefree, big joker demeanor. And what were these covers masking? We were all desperately struggling to hide our loneliness, our true feelings. Everyone sought some way to endure the personal, debilitating life circumstances.

The most helpful escape for me was to be top-side and alone very late at night or in the early morning. Being a radarman made it convenient to arrange those occasions for myself without being conspicuous. Radar watch had me awake when most of the crew was sleeping. After my period on watch was finished I often went out on the boat deck or up in the bow where I could be completely alone, simply soaking up the silence. A slight breeze, deliciously fresh air, no lights other than the stars and the moon. Nothing else was visible in any direction other than the ships in our convoy. They were positioned at intervals sufficiently far off that they did not intrude on my private space. Their presence in their positions added to the tranquility. It was like traveling with good friends, companions who are savoring the scene and the silence. That felt good. The only sound was that of our odd little ship slushing along through the water. We could not boast of slicing through the waves as did the powerful, handsome ships of the line. That did not matter. Those occasions surely helped keep my head straight

Watching a new destination emerge from the sea was always a spellbinding show. Moving slowly across the sea for a week, two weeks, never sighting land in any direction, certainly adds credence to the belief that one eventually comes to the end of the earth and falls off to infinity. Progress is seen only as it is penciled on the navigation charts. None of our officers had much experience in using a sextant or identifying celestial bodies, or operating the Loran gear, the new gadget for navigating. The consequence was a great deal of communicating with the other ships to compare notes on our position. But from the charts I could determine just about when I could begin searching ahead with long range radar capabilities for the tell-tale blip on the radar screen which was the electronic equivalent of a lookout up in the crow's nest of an ancient vessel shouting, "Land ho!" Visually, the horizon is but twelve to fourteen miles away. That is as far as the eye can see. With radar, even the primitive equipment we had, vision was extended significantly. Changing from the short range sweep of the radar used for "seeing" the other ships in our convoy, to a long distance search of sixty to eighty miles required only the flip of a switch. Radar could then peer far over the horizon and report back any indications of land ahead. When that blip appeared indicating land ahead, it was the moment to report the news to the skipper and the officer on watch in the conning tower.

The radar message revealing land just over the horizon was like the orchestra striking up the overture. It announced, "Curtain going up. Please take your seats everyone. The spectacular sights are about to begin." A captivating, enthralling show was about to begin. A new destination was about to come out of the sea, gradually revealing the details of its unique character. It was always a spectacular performance. At first it is but a dot on the horizon, a dot so obscure that you wonder if you are only imagining that you see it. A mirage perhaps. But no, there really is something out there. Gradually it grows, rising out of the sea, displaying more and more of itself, taking on detail. That which was a vague dot on the horizon comes alive. Dark, shapeless images become a million shades of green, brown, black, yellow. Slowly they separate themselves…Eventually specifics become discernible…trees, buildings, streets. At last vehicles and people appear. That is the crescendo. One begins to catch the dynamics of the place. It beckons. I can't wait to get ashore to discover, to explore, to interact with people and places and things, all of them new. The local food and possibly a little booze beckon. Who knows what else we can find? We reach the dock, tie up…We're here at last.

The Hawaiian Islands of Oahu and Molokai were sighted off the port bow on January 22, 1945. Somehow we had found our way to Hawaii. The immensity of the Pacific Ocean and the contrastingly insignificant size of the Hawaiian Islands and the relative inexperience of everyone on the 834 combined to provide plenty of opportunities for navigational errors. A modest miscalculation would have resulted in a major misdirection. Fortunately, that did not occur. By 11:30 A.M. we had moved into the harbor and moored at the Iriquoos Section, Pearl Harbor. Seeing the remains of ships that had been sunk by the Japanese had a predictable impact on everyone. There was our Navy, the old warships of the line, destroyed by the same enemy we were soon to encounter. Pay back time was approaching. The scene at Pearl Harbor sent a powerful message. Those immense ships setting on the bottom of the harbor made us realize the vulnerability of our fragile little amphibious vessel. But, on with our business. First, the dry cargo was removed from the 834. Then we moved to West Lock where 15,000 gallons of fuel oil were transferred to a barge. That done, thoughts turned to liberty in Honolulu.

In January, 1945, Honolulu was wall to wall sailors, soldiers, and marines. Even so, it was a very attractive liberty town. Maybe any town would look good after the long trek from San Diego. To escape the congestion of the central city, I hopped on a bus for Waikiki Beach, but a few minutes away. The beach was a surprise in that the sand was black, of volcanic origin. But the big surprise was that hardly anyone was there. The oceanfront street was a rather quiet, two lane affair lined with palm trees and modest residences. The view of the sea was gorgeous. A great place to live in peacetime if it could remain this way. Living there prior to World War II must have been the realization of an idyllic dream about the tropical, island life.

Another event I wanted to experience in Honolulu was to see Bobby Riggs. Riggs was the number one tennis player in the world in 1939. I had read that he was now fulfilling his military obligation on the tennis courts at the Royal Hawaiian Hotel. So, I hopped on another bus that delivered me to the gates of the hotel in a few minutes. The hotel and the adjacent tennis club were fabulous, but no Bobby Riggs. He had already been moved to a new assignment as the available tennis celebrity for the officers at Admiral Nimitz mountainside headquarters on Guam. Tough duty.

I got into a routine of volunteering for any working parties going ashore. That got me off the ship, gave me an opportunity to see a bit more of a place, and to steal a little food for my locker. Whenever the working party was going for food, it put me in a situation where we would go deep into the holds of ships to load cargo nets with crates and cartons of food. Out of sight, we could crack open cartons of fresh fruits and gorge ourselves on whatever was available. Pears, apples, oranges, canned juices, canned fruits...the works. Cargo nets lifted our legitimate provisions from the hold and onto our waiting boat. We in the working party would then climb ladders up and out of the hold, each of us with shirts stuffed with stolen merchandise. All of this required cooperation from men on the supply ship. It made no difference to them. Volunteering for the working party was a win-win situation. Everything to win and nothing to lose. I could never figure out why everyone in the crew didn't figure that out. Fortunately for me, they didn't.

Now and again the idea of volunteering for a working party backfired. It did at Pearl Harbor. A fellow named Ensign Broadbent, one of the two new officers who came aboard at San Diego, was essentially a gofer. His forte was foraging for goodies beyond the basic food requirements that the officers would find pleasing embellishments to their lives. Things like whiskey, ice cream, phonograph records; that sort of thing Broadbent would obtain by sniffing around here and there. I went along with him on one of his hunting expeditions at the Pearl Harbor supply depots. I was to carry the loot if Broadbent was successful in convincing a supply officer that his cause was just. On this occasion he failed. However,

he turned it into a bonanza afternoon for himself. He decided to

make the most of the situation by spending the afternoon at a nearby

officer's club. I tagged along. At the entrance to the club he explained

that because this was the exclusive domain of commissioned officers

I would have to wait for him on the porch steps. I sat on those steps

for three hours while my "superior" and his companions suffered

through the long afternoon in their opulent setting. I watched those

"superior" souls come and go, passing me without a hello or even

a glance. And why should they? They had been designated as a

cut above. I was to play the role of lesser being. The incident left

indelible marks on me. It was an illustration of military hierarchy at

its best. Or worst. Were we representatives of the same democracy?

Or had democracy been shelved for the duration? Sometimes the

working party just did not work out.

Chapter Fourteen
My Opportunity to be the Trigger Man

Firepower on the 834, as I have already specified, consisted of twelve twenty-millimeter anti-aircraft guns and seven forty-millimeter anti-aircraft cannons. Gun crews, organized on the shakedown cruise, went through frequent drills and practice sessions whenever we were at sea. My responsibility was to load and re-load and re-load and re-load one of the twenty-millimeter guns. My partner, the fellow who actually aimed and fired the gun, was a fellow from West Virginia named Parker. He was an excellent marksman, probably the best we had. All I had to do was stand by to remove the spent magazine and replace it with a fresh, fully loaded magazine. I was neither quick nor efficient at the task, but we managed. The ammunition was, to my way of lifting, extremely heavy. Holding one of the magazines steady long enough to fit it into the gun required more muscle than I possessed. With all the other guns firing at the same time, the situation was always damned disconcerting; definitely not my cup of tea. Cumbersome life jackets and metal helmets had to be worn at battle stations, too; making the task even more awkward. Compounding my difficulty was that I really did not like being around guns of any kind. Such a lousy warrior, I was.

On the first day out of Hawaii I had my first and last experience actually firing the twenty millimeter gun. What a fiasco that turned out to be. A special event had been arranged. A Navy fighter plane was to fly over us trailing a target. The target resembled an enormous shirtsleeve attached to a cable trailing behind the airplane. The object, of course, was to shoot the sleeve, not the airplane.

On this occasion my division officer was in the conning tower with the skipper. For some unexplainable reason, they made a decision (a decision they would soon deeply regret) to have me switch places with Parker. I was to become the trigger man. Parker and I were both perplexed, but did as directed; we switched places. A belt, sort of a girdle, held the gunner in place so he could lean back and maneuver the gun. Parker helped me get strapped into the firing position. Weight of the gunner against the supporting girdle served to counter-balance the forward weight of the gun. It involves utilization of a simple principle of physics. Nothing to it once you get the idea. As with persons on a teeter-totter balancing and counter-balancing each other, Gunner and gun could move up or down comfortably. I did not know that.

Nervous, excited, inept, untrained, I wrestled with the gun, fought against the physics of the task, making manipulation of the anti-aircraft gun an enormous struggle. Parker snapped a fresh magazine of tracer bullets into the gun. My body continued to fight against the correct use of weight and muscle. It was a clumsy struggle. Parker tried to ease my anxiety. He said, "Snuffy, ain't nuthin' to it. Just lean back and take it easy." In the next few seconds all hell broke loose. The airplane trailing the target sleeve came into view. "Commence firing, commence firing," came the command from the conning tower. I hauled the barrel of that twenty millimeter gun skyward and sent a barrage of tracer bullets in what I judged to be the direction of the passing sleeve. Boy oh boy, was I off target. I damn near shot down the airplane. "Cease firing, cease firing." shouted Captain Bentley. His agitation was certainly justified. I was promptly, permanently removed from my position as gunner. But that was not the end of it. The pilot of the airplane reported the incident to base headquarters. Captain Bentley received an immediate dressing down in a radio message from command at Naval Air Station, Oahu. After securing from the drill I was ordered to appear before the captain, who gave me a thorough verbal blasting, a one way communication which focused on my incompetence. My career as gunner ended as quickly as it had begun. That was fine with me. And Parker was happy to resume his role as the man with his finger on the trigger. Parker was a farm boy, a tall skinny guy. While he did not appear to be particularly muscular, he was actually a very strong fellow. We were destined to spend many, many hours, entire nights even, together at that gun station. He was a good storyteller, which turned what could have been dull, dragging hours into entertaining, interesting periods of

Parker sharing tales of his life in West Virginia. At Okinawa both

his stories and his marksmanship figured significantly in my life.

Chapter Fifteen
Jolly Roger Flies as we Cross the Equator

For eight days our course was southwest, heading for Funa Futi, a dot in the south Pacific Ocean. Days were very, very hot as we approached the equator. Many shipmates carried their mattresses topside at night in order to escape the stifling heat of our berthing compartments. The poor guys who were deck hands had to work like beasts in the sweltering equatorial sun, chipping paint, painting decks, sweeping decks. Bob Bright was one of those poor devils. He managed to turn the situation his way eventually, but on this occasion he turned his suffering into a great laugh. He and the other deck hands had been out in the sun all morning, When they were dismissed for chow at noon, Bob came walking into the mess compartment ringing wet with sweat and filthy dirty. All he was wearing were his shoes and shorts. His penis hanging out of his shorts completed his costume. He said, "If I'm gonna work like a dog I might just as well look like one." The incongruity broke everyone down. It was hilarious...Just what everyone needed. Bob was a smart fellow. He eventually figured out a way to get out from under Lichek and the first division by getting one of the yeomen to teach him how to type, yeoman style. Then he got Ensign Latz to take him on as a yeoman striker. From then on he was in clean clothes and working at a desk in the yeoman's suite. Yes, he was a smart, clever fellow.

Jolly Roger, a black flag emblazoned with skull and crossbones, replaced the American flag on February 5, 1945. We had reached latitude 00000 and longitude 176.40, the equator. It was a day devoted to silliness, to fun, to tomfoolery. On this day I, and my fellow Pollywogs, were initiated into the Solemn Mysteries of the Ancient Order of the Deep. According to the ancient lore of the sea, we had passed into the Royal Domain of Neptunus Rex, Ruler of the Raging Main. Officers and crew had to be inspected and passed on by Neptunus Rex and his Royal Staff. The inspection was a rite of passage all sailors submit to the first time they cross the equator. We Pollywogs, sailors who had never crossed the equator, had never entered the Domain of Neptunus Rex, were plentiful on the 834. Nonsense was organized by the small band of crewmen who had previously crossed the equator. They arranged for a grand initiation procedure. These men were known as Shellbacks. Starring in the role of King Neptune was a jovial fellow named Henry Hibbits. Henry ascended his makeshift throne and reigned over his kingdom with flair befitting this noble, frivolous ceremony. "Let the ceremonies begin," he announced quite regally. And begin, they did.

Tony Danapas was a Pollywog, just the same as me. Everyone but Danapas stayed in good spirits all through the nonsense of the hazings that day. Danapas, who always tried to exhibit himself as the tough, seasoned sailor, broke down that day in the most embarrassing manner. It was great fun for the rest of the crew, but Tony the Pollywog, took the events of the day as a threat to his status. That made his break down a delicious moment for everyone else. The situation was so devastating to his fragile ego that he broke down and cried. It was a huge bonus, a splendid boost to our morale to see him in tears in a simple circumstance. The incident haunted him from that day to the end of his stay of the 834. It was simply the threat of a haircut that brought him to tears. However, a whole lot happened before Tony boy sobbed.

Shellbacks were served a sumptuous breakfast in grand style, with fresh eggs, ham, pastries, fresh fruit, coffee...the works. Our breakfast consisted of half-cooked beans and cold coffee.

My first task after breakfast was to join my fellow Pollywogs in the third division for a clean sweep down of the boat deck using toothbrushes for our brooms. A number of Shellbacks stood over us, harassing us, cajoling us, finding fault with our effort. That task finished, a Shellback ordered me to fall in line with five other Pollywogs, all of us nonsmokers. We were escorted to the brig (the shipboard jail) and locked inside the iron bars. The brig was a tiny cubicle about four feet deep, eight feet wide, and six feet high. There was no outside ventilation. Each of us was handed a long black cigar. "Okay, Pollywogs, light up and smoke your cigars down to a one inch butt. You get out when everyone has his smoke down to a one inch butt, not before. Understand?" We all lit up and started puffing away. It was the first cigar of my life. In no time the brig was saturated with smoke. The assumption, of course, is that one or all of us would become ill, plead for mercy, beg to be released. Oddly enough, not one of us became ill; not even uncomfortable. I discovered that I genuinely enjoyed smoking that cigar. The temperature in such close quarters was the real bugaboo, but we managed just fine. The trick backfired. When the Shellback returned we submitted our one inch butts and were promptly released from captivity. But there was no slipping away. We were ushered topside for the haircut of haircuts.

Every Pollywog but one got a haircut from the Domain barber of the day. The designated barber had never before cut hair. He used a pair of tin snips, or wire cutters, to do the job. This situation produced some wild haircuts, but that was okay. What difference could it make? None, to anyone but Tony Danapas. His reaction was a surprise and it brought joy to everyone in ship's company. Tony was very quiet while waiting in line for his haircut. He kept drifting to the back of the line, avoiding the moment of confrontation with the barber, postponing his encounter with King Neptune's cutter. Ultimately his turn came. Shorn Pollywogs ringed the stool that served as the barber chair. The Shellback barber was about to do the job on Tony's black, greasy curls. That's when Tony began to weep. Macho Tony Danapas in tears over losing his curly locks. Then Tony lost it all. He backed away, doubled up his fist, and completely losing his judgment, threatened the bogus barber. "Damn you Russell, you ain't gonna mess up my hair," Tony shouted, all the time sobbing uncontrollably. There was no response to his threat, no effort to force the man to get his head clipped. Shipmates who had long been bossed around by Danapas were ecstatic. Witnessing Danapas fall apart over a simple prank did them a world of good. They would never let him forget this moment.

Next came a trip through the garbage, a total immersion in fact. A target sleeve, one of those sleeves that trailed behind the airplane I had fired at as we left Pearl Harbor, was spread across the main deck. I have no idea how we got hold of that sleeve, but it was the centerpiece of the next phase of our hazing. The sleeve had been filled with sloppy, slushy, smelly garbage held over from several days of discarded food from our mess. Pollywogs were lined up, then stuffed into the sleeve with orders to crawl on our hands and knees through the garbage to the other end. Somewhere along the dark journey a Shellback stationed above the sleeve shoved the passing Pollywogs flat down into the garbage. Having been fully soaked in the mushy mess, Pollywogs emerged from their tour of the sleeve garbage soaked, dripping everything from stewed tomatoes to coffee grounds.

Once out of the sleeve we were led to an improvised pool of salt water on the main deck. Although the salt water contained a good bit of floating garbage washed from the bodies of Pollywogs who had preceded me, the crude bath was a much appreciated amenity. It felt so good to have the garbage soak itself loose from my clothing and shoes. The smell hung on and the salt water brought a bit of discomfort, but, all things considered, the situation looked pretty good. But the event in the salt water bath was not yet complete. There was a bit more to come. I was soaking myself in the salt water bath when suddenly a Shellback had me by the back of the neck.

He stuffed my head under water and held me there until I thought my lungs would surely burst. Finally he pulled my head up into the fresh air and he shouted, ""Pollywog or Shellback?" Then down in the salt water went my head, again for what seemed an interminable period. Again, I was pulled from the water and asked the question, "Pollywog or Shellback?" Head thrust under water for the third time, the longest time of all. When my head was snapped once more to the fresh air I came up shouting, "Shellback, Shellback, God Damn it world, I am a Shellback!" A handshake, a pat on the back, and "Congratulations, Shellback Shannon. Now go and pay your respects to His Majesty, King Neptunus Rex."

Sitting on his throne was our king for the day, Henry Hibbits. He was a king Neptune right out of the story book. His skinny, bony legs, his round red face, his scraggly beard, his hairy chest, and his fat belly combined to produce the ideal Neptunus Rex. Naked except for his underwear and a paper crown, Henry squatted on his makeshift throne, holding as his scepter – a dirty mop.

A Shellback serving as King Neptune's page directed me to kneel before the king. I did so. It was the most ludicrous scene one could ever imagine. I raised my head to look at fat Henry Hibbits, my King Neptune. Suddenly I was grabbed by both ears and my nose was pushed into the flabby belly of King Neptune. His belly was covered with heavy grease, as thick as axle grease. My face was rubbed into that greasy belly of the king until much of the glop had been transferred to me. Finally, I heard the message. King Neptunus Rex touched my shoulders with his scepter, the wet, dirty mop, he exclaimed, "I dub you Shellback Shannon.

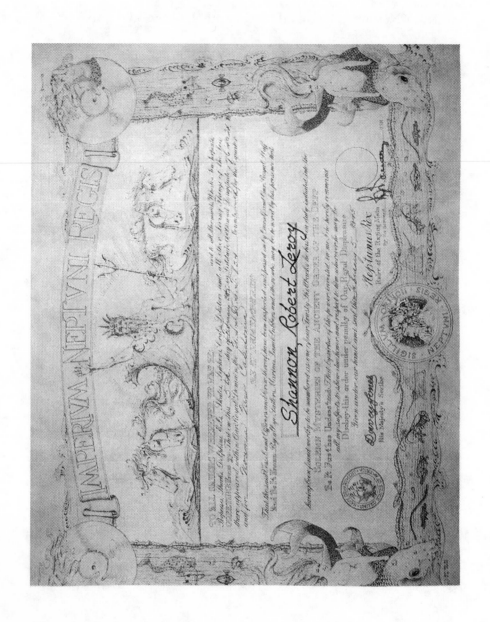

114

You are now a fully initiated member for life in the Solemn Mysteries of the Ancient Order of the Deep."

As soon as the revelry was completed, Jolly Roger came down and the American flag was returned to its place atop the mast. Regular routines resumed immediately after all Pollywogs had been welcomed to the Ancient Order of the Deep by King Neptunus Rex, including the humiliated Tony Danapas.

Continuing on a southwesterly course we crossed the International Date Line on February 7, 1945. Monotony and the unrelenting sun began to affect everyone. Tempers flared at the slightest provocation. Lichek showed no consideration or compassion for the deck hands. He saw to it that Danapas kept them working in the intense heat, forcing them to suffer under the equatorial sun. Inevitably, shipmates became irritated with each other. Lichek's unreasonableness took its toll.

A dispute over an electric fan in the mess compartment ended up in a bit of a brawl. It happened at lunchtime. Bernard Minear, a deck hand, a coxwain and a marvelous fellow was one of the first to enter the mess compartment that day. He set his tray of food on a table and turned the electric fan in his direction in order to get the little bit of cooling effect it provided. A six inch fan trying to give some relief from the stifling heat of that compartment was an impossible endeavor. Bernard was all set, but it was of no help to most of the sweat-soaked sailors sitting with him at the table. The tiny fan had no oscillating capability. One direction. That was it. The mess compartment soon filled with ill-tempered crewmen. Wilmore, an obnoxious bastard, was the last to enter. With no more space available at the table where Bernard was sitting, Wilmore set his tray of food on the adjacent table, turned the fan in his direction, and sat down. Bernard got up and re-directed the fan his way. Without comment, Wilmore reached up and with his fork flipped the fan back toward himself. Again, Minear turned the modest breeze to his benefit. Wilmore retaliated. This time Bernard slammed the fan back to where he could enjoy it. Still standing, using his fork as a pointer, Bernard shouted, "Wilmore, you son-of-a-bitch, I was here first, I set that fucking fan to blow on us and that's just where that fucking fan is going to stay." Wilmore said nothing. He re-directed the fan toward himself. That did it. Bernard, a tall, powerful man, pulled Wilmore from his place on the bench and literally threw him onto the mess table. Mess trays went flying as Wilmore slid the full length of the table on his back. Bernard grabbed him a second time, pinned him to the deck and pummeled him. It was no contest. Shipmates pried Bernard away or I believe he would have killed the man. Wilmore left the mess compartment without saying a word.

Oliveto assured his friend Minear that Wilmore would not report the incident to anyone. "He knows better than to do anything like that. We'd all be after his ass if he did and he knows it." Others reinforced what Oliveto said. Everyone pitched in to clean the mess compartment.

Wilmore stayed clear of Bernard Minnear at all times thereafter. The incident demonstrated how the relentless heat, the joyless existence, the apprehensions and uncertainties about the near future and what was going to happen to us were affecting every man on board the 834.

I, too, became impatient with a shipmate one night. In all my life I tried to avoid fights, because I always came out on the short end. Being a half-pint doesn't put a guy in for very good odds. I was that half-pint. The guy who slept in the middle bunk straight across from mine, Melvin Brinson, got to me. Lights were still on. I was in my bunk reading. Melvin started messing around, tickling me. I told him a dozen times to quit. He didn't. I rolled out of my bunk and nailed him square on the jaw with my good old left fist. Melvin crawled into his bunk. He stayed there for several days, living on a liquid diet. But, nobody reported the incident to an officer. An unwritten code among the crew prevailed. Silence. Nothing happened to me. Melvin never bothered me again.

Humiliations brought on by the cast system that existed on the 834 were difficult for me to endure. There were some canvas backed folding chairs on the boat deck. Emblazoned across those canvas backs were the words OFFICERS ONLY. Oh, boy how that bugged me. How close I came to throwing those chairs over the side. OFFICERS ONLY....Real democracy. I didn't get much out of history courses in high school, but I remember one picture in particular. It was in a section of the history book which dealt with the treatment of Irish immigrants to the United States. A Shannon can be pretty sensitive about anything derogatory to the Irish. The picture showed a very ordinary looking saloon. In the window of the saloon was a sign that read, NO DOGS OR IRISH ALLOWED. In my mind there was not a bit of difference between that and OFFICERS ONLY.

One day we were subjected to an inspection of our lockers. Something of Captain Bentley's was missing. I can't remember what it was. Nevertheless, I was required to open my locker and stand beside it while division officer Dillon searched through the little bit of private storage that was mine. He emptied the locker, one item at a time, tossed the contents onto my bunk, and left me to put the stuff back where he had found it. Every shipmate got the same treatment. Whatever the skipper was looking for was not found. But the exercise surely furthered a disdain for "superior officers."

On another occasion, while we were at Guam, Dillon accused me of stealing his khaki pants from the laundry room and cutting them off to make the shorts I was wearing. I was standing outside the wheelhouse when he broached the matter. He insisted that I take the khaki shorts off so he could check to see if his name was stenciled inside. I took off the shorts for the stencil inspection by my "superior." No stencil. I had picked up those pants at a Marine supply depot on Guam. Dillon returned my shorts. He offered no apology. In his presence I threw them into the sea. To have to take that kind of bullshit and not be able to do anything about it was the most difficult aspect of Navy life for me. The degradations, the indignities, the humiliations inherent in the cast system that prevailed on the 834—they were real tough to take.

Funa Futi Island did nothing to boost our sagging spirits. We anchored in the lagoon a few hundred yards off shore on February 9, 1945. A ring-like coral reef, a mere atoll, Funa Futi looked to us like it was barely habitable. But it was home for some poor souls. The 834 was soon surrounded by rather primitive boats holding natives begging for whatever we would throw them—candies, cigarettes, even garbage. They appeared to be a sickly lot. Maybe they were perfectly healthy, but they certainly did not look at all prosperous.

The natives kept their boats very close to the 834. All of them except one, that is. One native boat pulled away from our stern and headed for shore. That was noticeable, but of no special concern or interest to anyone. In about half an hour the same boat returned, again maneuvering to our stern. Hidden from the view of officers in the conning tower, Davey Shaeffer crawled out from beneath a blanket, climbed the stern ladder on the 834, and went below deck to shower. Davey had negotiated with one of the natives to take him ashore for a quick screw and a return to the ship. Slick as can be, Davey pulled it off while the rest of us pitched junk foods to the natives. He was the only man to go ashore at Funa Futi. None of the officers ever discovered what he had done. Good for Davey. But three days later he had another dose of the clap. It was always the same. Wherever we landed, Davey would figure out a way to get off the ship to get laid. Always he would get the clap, but that was no deterrent. Funa Futi was no exception.

Everyone liked Davey, a curly headed, mischievous little fellow. He was a cook, a good one. And, with good reason, he was a very nervous guy. Off the Italian coast he was blown into the sea when his previous ship was destroyed by the Germans. His hands trembled uncontrollably all the time. Davey performed a neat trick with cigarettes. He'd place one in the palm of his hand, slap the wrist of that hand, and the cigarette would flip end over end and settle between his lips ready for lighting. I watched him do that a

million times. Davey was a special kind of fellow.

Chapter Sixteen
Woods is Caught with His Pants Down and His Mouth Full

Next day we were underway at dawn, en route to Noumea, New Caledonia. Chart room publications gave some encouraging information on the potential of Noumea as a good liberty town. The prospect of engaging in the delights of a French settlement after this long period at sea in the miserable equatorial heat surely was appealing. But that was five days away, plenty of time for shenanigans. Hardly a day passed without someone unwittingly becoming the center of some ridiculous, but hilarious situation. Hilarious, that is, for everyone except the guy who was the butt of the happening. And it didn't go away. The poor guy had to contend with references to the incident from then on.

The head on the 834 was a place where lots of funny things happened. Each head contained three toilets, two urinals, four showerheads, and six or eight sinks. No partitions, of course, so the head was the center of much sociability for every occasion, including sitting on the toilet.

Now and then Amos and I had to do a week of keeping the head clean. Sailing between Funa Futi and New Caledonia our turn came up. Amos was good at that, too. I was satisfied just giving the place a lick and a promise, but not Amos. Like he did everything, he gave the head a thorough cleaning. Two funny things happened during that week. There was always a steady stream of shipmates coming and going in the head. Sometimes they came because of a legitimate need to visit the urinal or the toilet, but frequently the visit was an excuse to goof off for as long as possible. When we knew Lichek was about to come through on an inspection tour we would make everyone clear out in order to keep the place spotless. Other times there was no need to close down the head while we cleaned, because it needed to be available without interruption for obvious reasons. So there were shipmates coming and going and hanging around while Amos and I cleaned. The heavy traffic produced two memorable incidents.

A fellow by the name of Gremels, a fat, obnoxious ship fitter, was a few years older than most of the crewmates. He tried to pass himself off as a man of great wisdom and accomplishment. He worked hard at being refined and sophisticated, but just could not pull it off. The guy was a joke, a transparent, laughable character. John Penn, the wild kid who thrived on mischief, dissolved Gremels' façade with a masterful one-liner delivered with perfect timing. It was situation comedy at its best. Amos and I were busy cleaning. A couple of guys were just hanging around. Gremels came into the head and went directly to the urinal to pee. John Penn went to the urinal next to where Gremels was standing. John seized the moment. He shouted, "Hey look fellas, Gremi's got one too!" Everyone relished the situation but Gremels. Indignant at such an affront, he quickly buttoned his pants and disappeared. Good old John Penn could always deliver the unexpected.

125

The second incident involved a chubby little storekeeper named Woods. Storekeepers had good duty. Their work was essentially clean and light. Best of all for storekeepers was that they controlled access to and distribution of food. They kept the records and maintained the inventory of all our food supplies, and they had the keys to where the food was stored. Woods, anytime day or night, wherever he was, whatever he was doing, was eating something. He had no sense of discretion, no consideration of his shipmates. Always he was munching on an apple or an orange or an egg sandwich or something like that. It was the kind of food every man longed for but could not obtain. Woods was a nice fellow, but he had this one terribly bad habit. He gave the impression, perhaps unwittingly, that he was deliberately flaunting his access to food. Poole, a ship fitter, was especially disgusted with Woods and his conspicuous consumption of extra rations. One day in the head Poole stumbled onto the opportunity to nail Woods forever. Approaching the urinal, Poole glanced into the toilet area. He spied Woods sitting on the toilet eating a sandwich. Immediately Poole called out, "Straus, Shannon, come in here right away. You're not gonna believe this unless you see it." We stepped over to where Poole was standing, both hands on his hips, shaking his head in disbelief. There was Woods, sitting on the toilet, trousers and underwear down around his ankles, sandwich in his hand, chewing on a bite of it while simultaneously taking a shit. Several more shipmates came in when they heard us laughing. Woods found himself with an audience glaring at him. What an embarrassing predicament he had arranged for himself. He had to wipe his ass with one hand, hold the sandwich with the other, pull up his underwear and trousers some way, get himself buttoned up and get out of there, all the while enduring the taunts of shipmates enjoying his dilemma. One fellow began what immediately became a chorus of "Oink, oink, oink." Poor Woods slunk away, absorbing humiliating jeers from shipmates. No one ever let him forget that day. Other than at mess with a tray of food identical to that of everyone else, no one ever saw Woods with extra food again. I am sure he continued to feast on extra rations of fresh fruits and such, but we never saw it again.

Inspection of the head by my nemesis, Ensign Lichek, was the main event for Amos and me on the final day of our week cleaning the damn place. We had it looking great. The place was spotless. When Lichek arrived, Amos was standing at one entrance and I was standing at the other, refusing to admit anyone until the inspection was completed. Lichek meticulously examined every inch and every aspect of that head. He could find no fault. As he departed, almost as an afterthought, a parting gesture, he checked behind the big hot water heater. Reaching as far as his long arm would permit, he ran his finger along the surface of the bulkhead and the water heater. His desperate search for dust paid off. He found plenty. No one had cleaned behind that water heater since it was installed back in Pittsburgh. Lichek stuck his dust covered finger under my nose. "You call that clean, Shannon? Yes, I suppose you would. It's filthy, that's what it is, filthy. Danapas, give Shannon ten hours extra duty, every minute of it cleaning this head. Shannon, you figure out how to clean behind that water heater or you'll be doing extra duty as long as you and I are on this ship." Amos pointed out that he was equally responsible. Lichek would have none of it. He and his sycophant left. That dose of extra duty meant that I was restricted to the ship. Thanks to Lichek, there would be no liberty for me in New Caledonia.

Chapter Seventeen
The Missing Morphine

Somewhere between Funa Futi and New Caledonia, Pappy Partin, an inveterate liar and schemer, came down with a mysterious illness. His bunk, the bottom one, was directly beneath mine. Because he was in his bunk most of the time, I did not regard it as unusual when he began sacking out more frequently. He was a truly feckless individual in the eyes of everyone except our division officer, Ensign Dillon. Partin had effectively pulled the wool over Dillon's eyes. The man was devious; clever in a self-serving way.

At daybreak, two days before we reached New Caledonia, I shut down the radar and went to my bunk. Partin was in his bunk groaning and moaning pitifully. Responding to my inquiry as to what was wrong, Partin explained that he was sick to his stomach. He thought he was dying. Our conversation and Partin's moaning awakened others who were less concerned about Pappy Partin's health than they were about being cheated out of a few minutes of sleep. "Knock it off, God damn it. Get the hell out of here if you want to talk," were the concerned comments from crewmates. I wanted to fall into my own sack for a few hours, but no one could sleep with Partin making such a fuss. I told him to quiet down while I went for the pharmacist mate. Rousing McCord, the pharmacist mate, was no problem. Without hesitation he slid out of his bunk and into some clothes. I helped him get Partin to sick bay, returned to my bunk and fell asleep.

Partin's condition did not improve. By the time we reached New Caledonia on February 14th, Pappy was receiving the royal treatment. He was relieved of all duties. Pharmacist mates checked on him several times a day. They put him on a special diet. Fresh eggs and fruit every morning. His midday and evening meals of soups and mild dishes were individually prepared and brought to him. He left his bunk only for the toilet, the shower, and for fresh air topside in the cool of the night. Pharmacist mates were unable to identify what was ailing the man. No one else on board was showing any symptoms similar to Partin's. It was, indeed, a mysterious malady.

Partin missed out on liberty in New Caledonia. The only other fellow who missed out on that liberty was me. Thanks to Ensign Lichek, I spent my liberty time in the bilges with a paint brush while my shipmates cavorted with the French girls in Noumea. The closest I got to the city was a view from where we docked along the embankment at the end of Avenue de la Victoire. The city known as the Pearl of the Pacific beckoned, but I did not get ashore.

Tanks, landing vehicles, and personnel we had transported from Hawaii were unloaded, our fresh water supply replenished, and we were ready to leave New Caledonia; this time our destination was Guadalcanal in the Solomon Islands. A brief stop there to refuel and take on a supply of food and we were off again, traveling on to the Russell Islands. There we took on ammunition, Marines of the First Division, and some LVTs (Landing Vehicle Tanks). The LVT was a clumsy, vulnerable, amphibious, topless iron box designed to transport troops and supplies from the deck of an LST, across a few hundred yards of water and onto the beach. They were vulnerable both to the water and mortar fire. But they were to be the containers taking troops from the 834 to action against the Japanese. At the Russell Islands invasion rehearsals were conducted all day every day and into the night. All hands were involved in the complex exercises. Commands and demands intensified. Perhaps it was anxiety and fear of what was ahead, perhaps it was fatigue, but whatever the causes, nerves became frayed and tempers exploded. Sick call brought ever-increasing numbers of crewmen and Marines suffering from diarrhea, headaches, stomach discomfort and such. Sick? Yes, truly ill, and in most every case the illnesses could have a psychosomatic origin. Still, no one on the 834 knew that the where and when of the next major assault on the Japanese was set for Okinawa, April 1, 1945. And Pappy Partin? No change.

On every LST first aid kits were kept at the gun stations, in the engine room, and in the galley. In each of the first aid kits, morphine syrettes were among the supplies. Each syrette contained a dose of morphine attached to a hypodermic needle. Morphine, a pain killer extracted from opium, could have an obvious attraction as more than a painkiller. Our pharmacist mates made periodic checks of the contents of every first aid kit to insure that they were in proper order, ready for use at all times. Soon after leaving Pearl Harbor it was discovered that morphine syrettes were disappearing from first aid boxes at the gun stations. Only the pharmacist mates and the person stealing the morphine knew of this situation. It was a baffling mystery. Then came the "Aha, we've got it! It's Pappy Partin, just as sure as anything. Now , how do we catch him with the morphine?"

We returned to Guadalcanal where the intensity of invasion procedures was raised another notch. Over and over again the marines drove their clumsy vehicles out through our bow doors, down the ramp and into the water where they took positions in line and proceeded to the beach. Our two boats went through similar maneuvers with marines climbing down rope ladders into the boats and onto the beach. All other crewmen were at battle stations. These were full blown drills involving everyone except Pappy Partin. He stayed in his bunk.

Then one morning I was idly messing about in my locker when a pharmacist mate came to Partin's bunk. Partin was in the shower at the time, watched over by another pharmacist mate who was there to guarantee that Partin did not return to his bunk too soon. The game was on. The pharmacist mate searched through Partin's pants. "Shannon," he said, "you did not see me do this. Okay?" I nodded in assent. He then rejoined his partner in the shower room. A few minutes later they returned with Partin who wore only a towel around his waist. Partin reached for his jeans, but was told to hold on a minute. Both pharmacist mates examined Partin's palms, forearms, and the calves of his legs. The two looked at each other, nodding in concurrence at what they had seen and what they had concluded. The telltale evidence was clear. Needle marks. Next, the evidence was pulled from the pocket of Partin's jeans; a still packaged morphine syrette, and held under Partin's nose. "Partin, ever since we left Pearl Harbor you've been stealing these from the first aid kits at the gun stations." Partin responded, "No, Doc, that's not true. I've been sick, real sick, you know that." The Pharmacist mate took hold of Partin's hand, turned it palm up, showed him the needle marks on his forearm and hand. "Okay, Doc, it's true. But, I had to do something for the pain, I've been so sick." No luck. The pharmacist mate immediately reported his findings to Abercrombie, the executive officer. As soon as we anchored Partin was taken to a hospital ship. I never saw him again. Maybe he was the wisest man of all. He was returned to the United States and, I presume, dishonorably discharged. No more Navy, no more war for that lying, conniving bastard. He never had to atone for all that he had done and not done while aboard the 834. And he escaped unharmed. So, on we go. Back to the Russell Islands for a short stay and the forming up of the convoy that would take us on the next leg of our journey to war against the Japanese. This could be the last leg of the journey.

Chapter Eighteen
Ulithi Rendezvous

No more dress rehearsals. Ready or not, on March 12, 1945, we were one of a large group of ships that sailed northwest from Guadalcanal. After eleven days at sea, traveling through a region where the threat of attack by Japanese submarines and airplanes was constant, we anchored at Ulithi in the Caroline Islands. The scene was astonishing; ships of all kinds visible as far as the eye could see. And beyond that were a vast number of vessels serving as a picket line to intercept any Japanese attacks. Captain Bentley went to a command ship for a complete briefing on Operation Iceberg, the label given to this operation. Upon his return all hands were called together to learn details of the venture. He announced that we were to be involved in the invasion of Okinawa on Sunday, April 1, 1945. Okinawa? Where in the world is Okinawa? Bentley attempted to explain its location and a few facts about the island, but no one had the slightest comprehension of what he was talking about.

Rear Admiral Reifsnider, commander of amphibious forces that were to hit the northern half of the Okinawa beaches, had been at Pearl Harbor since November 24, 1944, planning the invasion. Information Captain Bentley received at the command ship had been put together by the Reifsnider staff. That information was placed on the chart table next to the radar gear. It helped me understand something about Okinawa and the invasion plans. Okinawa is the principal island among a group of 140 islands known as the Ryukus. It is approximately 60 miles long with a general orientation northeast to southwest. Maximum breadth of 18 miles is in the northeast where the topography is mountainous and heavily wooded. About 800,000 people, most of them farmers, lived on the island. Naha, the principal city, and the nearby airfields were early objectives in the invasion plan. A week of air strikes by B-29 bombers and carrier-based planes, combined with extensive naval bombardments preceded our arrival.

Continual attacks from the immense Japanese air power close to Okinawa was considered a certainty. U.S. reconnaissance reports estimated 2,000 to 3,000 airplanes at 65 airfields on Formosa and 55 airfields on Kyushu. Okinawa, but 350 miles from the Japanese home islands, was surely going to put us in their own backyard.

Eight transport squadrons carried our troops to Okinawa. Each squadron consisted of 15 assault transports, 6 cargo ships, 25 LSTs (Landing Ship Tank), and 10 LSMs (Landing Ship Medium). One segment of the armada would strike along five miles of beaches on the coast of southern Okinawa. The intention was to surprise the Japanese by faking an invasion on the eastern shore, round the southern tip of the island, and make the actual assault on the western shore Hagushi beaches. Immediate objectives once ashore were the two airfields near the Hagushi beaches, Yontan and Kadena. Securing Yontan was the first responsibility of the marines aboard the 834. Amphibious forces for the invasion numbered 1213 ships and 45 different types of landing craft. The 187 LSTs in this invasion fleet were acclaimed by the high level planners as "handy, ubiquitous, and greatly wanted."

A beer party, sort of a last supper, was our big event on March 22. Mogmog Beach was the site for our fiesta. Mogmog Beach. The name tells all about it. Mogmog Beach for the enlisted men. And for the officers? Here is what Samuel Eliot Morison wrote:

"Lagoon and atoll presented an astonishing appearance on 20 March. In addition to 40 or 50 ships that flew British ensigns, several hundred vessels of the United States Navy and Merchant Marine were present. Mogmog, the former seat of the king of Ulithi, transformed into a recreation center, was so full of bluejackets in shoregoing whites that from a distance it looked like one of those Maine islands where seagulls breed; one could hardly walk a step ashore without kicking an empty beer can. On the headquarters island, Commodore O. O. Scrappy Kessing, atoll commander, was dispensing characteristic hospitality at the crowded officers club, to the officers of the fleet and nurses from the three hospital ships present, Solace, Relief, and Comfort.

Some of these courageous ladies had their last dance

on this occasion, except their dance of death with the

Kamikaze boys."

In my next lifetime, when it comes time for me to go to war, I will

be sure to go as a commissioned officer, if only for the perquisites.

But this time the bon voyage party for my shipmates and me was

warm beer directly from the can on Mogmog Beach. Whoopee!

A final briefing occurred on March 23 when an officer from the

command ship came aboard. Gloom and doom were the dominant

themes of his briefing. His emphasis was on the vulnerability of

the LST to any Japanese naval vessel or aircraft that succeeded in

breaking through the ring of ships protecting us on the perimeter

of the invasion fleet. If they succeeded in breaking through, he

explained, we would be indefensibly vulnerable to attack by fast

moving torpedo boats, one-man submarines, and Kamikazes. If the

weather was good and the skies clear we would, in all probability,

be in for all-out attacks by Japanese airplanes based on Formosa,

Okinawa, and the Japanese home islands. He warned that attack

probabilities increased significantly as we closed the range for enemy forces. His closing shot: "The prospects are grim. I wish you Godspeed."

The next day a chaplain came aboard. He possessed all the essential credentials; a Christian, of course, a commissioned officer, of course, and he carried a polished communion server. He finished things off with a prayer for our survival and success against the enemy. Great stuff, I suppose. At least the chaplain felt that it was great stuff. His mission complete, the chaplain hopped into his waiting boat and was taxied to the next ship on his list. Business was good for the chaplain that day. He was in chaplain's heaven, praying everyone through. He was a real-for-sure sea-going circuit rider. Having an inside track to the almighty, the chaplain knew that we, being the good guys, had God on our side.

It is fascinating the way the world's warriors have always called on some brand of supreme something or other to see them through safely and to victory in battle. Annihilating the enemy because "our cause is just" is an aspect of the functioning of that God, too. In situations where each side is appealing to the same God, that supreme being is really put in a bind. God weighs the matter, selects a favorite, does the other guy in. The victor thanks his God. The loser cries out, "Hey God, what's the big idea?" The answer? God's will. Might, plus intervention by a loving God, spells victory. If we could just get word to the enemy, before the fighting starts, that God is on our side, we wouldn't need to go through all of this nonsense of shooting and killing. And, other than paying the salaries of a large batch of well paid chaplains, no military budget required. Such cynical idealism notwithstanding, the reality was that there, in the lagoon off Ulithi, we had a last communion before sailing off to kill some Japanese. Go get 'em boys!

Chapter Nineteen
The Greatest Easter Parade in History

Skies were overcast as we departed Ulithi on March 25, 1945.

Low hanging clouds covered us like a blanket. The sea was a bit

choppy, which made for some difficulty maintaining our position in

relation to the ships ahead and astern, as well as staying on course.

However, weather conditions were just what the doctor ordered. Or

was it the chaplain? God on our side? It surely looked that way.

Weather conditions remained the same right on through March 31,

precisely what we needed to discourage, perhaps prevent, those

anticipated assaults by the Japanese. None occurred; not a single

Japanese attack on any of the ships in our flotilla happened between Ulithi and Okinawa.

Skies cleared on the afternoon of March 31, and there it was, Okinawa, just off our starboard bow. But where were the Japanese? Assuming attack was imminent, all ships stood at general quarters, waiting for action. There were no attacks from the air, no Japanese ships, no shellings from shore batteries...nothing. Unmolested, the 834, along with every other ship in our group, continued toward pre-invasion positions. We were about to participate in the biggest, most unusual, Easter parade in history.

Thanks to Admiral Turner, a sheltered anchorage had already been secured for use by seaplanes, tankers, ammunition ships, and repair ships. Kerama Retto, a cluster of small mountainous islands just to the south of Okinawa had been invaded successfully in a daring-do venture. Turner's plan was strongly opposed by others at the strategic planning sessions, but he persisted and won out. He was right. The plan turned out to be a brilliant piece of military planning. Estimates of Japanese opposition at Kerama Retto had been greatly exaggerated by those opposing Turner's plan.

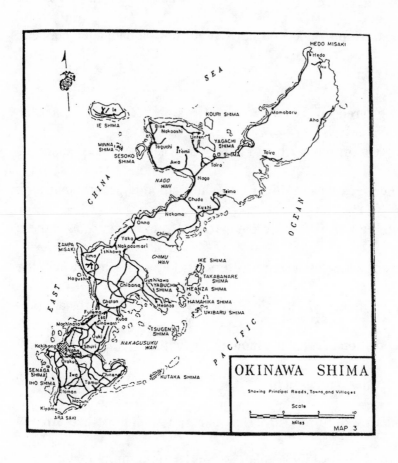

OKINAWA SHIMA

Showing Principal Roads, Towns, and Villages

Scale

Miles

MAP 3

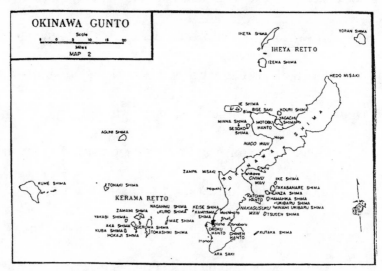

OKINAWA GUNTO

Scale

Miles

MAP 2

Five of the larger islands in the group were invaded on March 26, Palm Sunday. By afternoon of that day they were under American control. The decision to take Kerama Retto most certainly meant salvation for many U.S. ships. More than 250 Japanese suicide boats were found, well hidden and ready to go. Had they been free to intercept our task force we would have been sitting ducks. A lucky punch? Perhaps. Nonetheless, Turner's sense of knowing the right move to make saved a lot of American lives and got the invasion off to a great start. By March 31, seaplanes and their tenders were operational, and 35 ships were in the harbor ready to supply fuel, ammunition, and repairs.

At 0600 April 1, 1945, Easter Sunday, we arrived at our pre-invasion position with all hands at general quarters, ready to meet the enemy. Before that day ended we would learn that the Japanese were but one of the enemies we had to cope with in Operation Iceberg. We were somewhat prepared for the Japanese, however, the other assailants took us completely by surprise and very nearly did us in.

Easter Sunday was surely an unlikely day to engage the enemy. But there we were, in the midst of an armada heretofore unmatched in size and firepower. Weather-wise, conditions were perfect. Clear skies, calm seas, no wind; an ideal day for the amphibious forces to form up and launch the grandest, most unusual Easter parade of all time, a parade to the Hagushi beaches at Okinawa.

In their book, Typhoon of Steel, James and William Belotes described the scene this way:

"Combat had offered no similar spectacle since the mass charges of the French knights in the Hundred Years' War. Here was the finest moment in the history of amphibious operations: an almost unbroken line of landing craft eight miles long, simultaneously approaching one beach. With their armored prows pushing curling bow waves like manes, the propellers churning waves like flowing white tails, the amphtracts became the cataphracts of modern warfare. 'Can it be coincidence,' mused the U.S. Navy's great historian, Rear Admiral Samuel Eliot Morison, 'that the companion craft for beach Purple 1 is numbered 1066?"

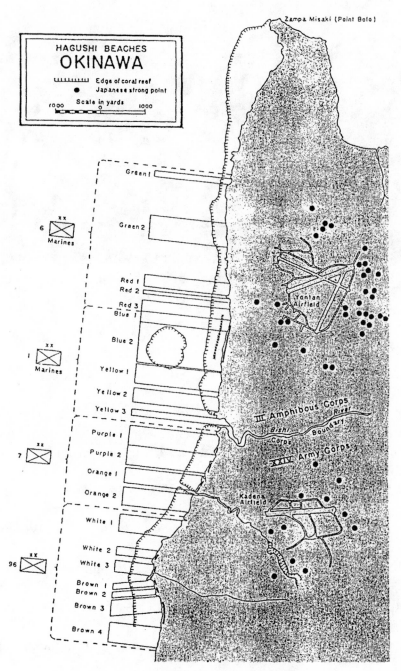

We hit at Hagushi's Blue Beach

LST 834 approaching the Hagushi beaches for the invasion of
Okinawa, April 1, 1945

The massive bow doors of the 834 were opened, the ramp lowered.
Marines made their way down the ladders to the tank deck and into
the amphtracs. Engines of the amphtracs came to life. The noise
of all those engines roaring in the vast hollow of our tank deck was
maddening. At precisely 0730 the amphtracs loaded with marines of
the first division drove down our ramp and into the water. Without a
hitch or hesitation they immediately formed in columns, just as they
had in the countless rehearsals. No mock invasion this time. Fully
aware that it was the Japanese homeland they were attacking, the

marines headed for the Hagushi Beach. The invasion of Okinawa was under way.

The moment the last of the amphtracs was on its way, ramp and bow doors on the 834 were closed and we got underway. We moved only a short distance southwest to what was referred to as the Outer Transport Area. It was a busy place. Hundreds of ships of every size, shape, and function, and each one a beehive of activity. On the 834 it was time to launch the Landing Craft Tank that had been riding piggyback on our main deck all the way from New Orleans. Dumping the LCT off our main deck and into the sea required the application of simple principles of physics and gravity, a neat little operation. The LCT was 160 feet long and 31 feet wide, an ocean-going craft of enormous weight. First off, of course, all the chains and blocks holding it in place had to be removed. Once that task was completed, seawater was pumped into the ballast tanks of the 834, starboard side, causing the ship to list; that is, to tilt. When the listing reached a critical point the LCT slid down well greased wooden beams on which it rested and plopped into the sea. The entire event went off smoothly, without a single mishap. We had grown so accustomed to life with the LCT in our midst that when it disappeared from view the main deck seemed naked. Seeing that landing craft drop away from its mother was like we had been pregnant and at last given birth to a new baby. It immediately took on a life of its own. Without champagne or ceremony, fifteen crewmen and one officer boarded the LCT, cranked up its engines and took off. The mission of the LCT began. It was put to work ferrying supplies, equipment, ammunition, fuel, and food to the beaches.

Before another hour had passed we had moored alongside the battleship Idaho. Talk about an incongruity; the LST 834 tied up to the Idaho was like the ugly duckling snuggled against the powerful, handsome prince. Or was she a queen? Our cargo for the Idaho was five inch shells. Transferring those shells from one ship to the other was extremely hazardous duty. But what if the Japanese attacked the Idaho while we were attached? Luck was with us. No Japanese appeared. The ammunition was transferred without incident. We immediately detached from the Idaho. There were other deliveries to make.

We served as a sea-going Wells Fargo wagon. Moor alongside a supply ship, take on cargo, beach and unload, pull away from the beach, attach to another supply ship; it was a vast miscellany, an unpredictable assignment.

Blue Beach, located on the northern half of the Hagushi beaches, was next for the 834. We beached, opened the bow doors, lowered the ramp, and for the next five days delivered the tools of war. It was an opportunity for me to slip away from the ship and do a little exploring. On the morning of the second day I strolled down the ramp and off the ship, just like I knew what I was doing. Nobody screamed "Halt, who goes there," or "Hey kid, where the hell do you think you are going?" I simply wandered away. It was a wonderful feeling. But I found myself in the midst of a wonderful chaos. Trucks and jeeps were going every which way imaginable. Maybe there was some kind of system in operation, but it seemed chaotic to me. Probably that is why nobody paid any attention to me as I meandered along. I noticed, up in the adjoining hillsides, a vast number of concrete structures. Intrigued, I went to have a closer look. It was a stupid idea, of course. They were perfect places for a Japanese soldier to

153

hole up for a few days while figuring out a scheme for getting out of his predicament. Nevertheless, off to the hills I went. Once in front of the small buildings, I had to go inside to see what I could find. I found bones. I was inside a burial tomb. The tomb contained rows of vases, each one containing human bones. But there was another occupant; an enormous spider was heading my way. That ended my investigation. I made a quick exit from the tomb, leaving the spider and its companions their private space.

I returned to the ship in one piece, but still wondering about the tombs. On the chart table I found a small publication about Okinawa which included a bit on the burial tombs. They were family burial tombs, located in that particular hillside because it faced west, toward China, the motherland. A concrete slab at the entrance to the tomb is where a family member's body is placed at death. The body remains there for three years, then it is placed in an urn inside the tomb. In my ignorance I had committed a sacrilege, a desecration. The spider did a good thing by running me off. One more point on those burial tombs that I read in the government publication was a warning to U.S. military personnel to be cautious because the tombs might be used as machine gun emplacements. It was really a dumb

move on my part, however, no harm done..

Chapter Twenty
Kamikazes Nonstop

Sporadic attacks by Japanese aircraft kept us at gun stations every night, all night. Everyone had some kind of duty day and night. During the first week of April, 1945, sleep was on everyone's mind. Parker, my mate at the portside amidship 20 millimeter anti-aircraft gun, could fall asleep anywhere. He had an incredible capability of relaxing, staying loose. He could fall asleep while fastened into the harness of that gun, but, in an instant, he would waken and be ready to fire at enemy aircraft. An amazing characteristic. Behind us on the main deck there was a cargo net filled with blocks of TNT. The cargo net became my place for taking a snooze. A few feet beyond the cargo net were barrels of gasoline waiting to be delivered ashore.

The TNT and gasoline made a happy combination for blowing us to kingdom come, whether it was a Kamikaze or "friendly fire" from the ships surrounding us. But the situation was not alarming in any way. I guess we must have assumed that nothing bad could happen to us; that we were impervious to the damage that could come our way.

The invasion of Okinawa was no surprise to the Japanese. On March 20, 1945, the Japanese high command had issued a directive specifying the Ryukus as the place they would need to defend next. They were well aware of U.S. invasion intentions, even though they might not have known precisely where we would attack in force. Their strategy was to not make a major effort to repulse the initial landings. Why that strategy? There are many imponderables which factored into the Japanese decisions. The effects of pre-invasion bombardments, the sinking of numerous Japanese troop ships bound for Okinawa, the increased and highly effective air strikes on the Japanese home islands, and the inevitable differences of opinion among the Japanese high command regarding strategy and tactics all influenced how the Japanese would proceed militarily.

Operation Ten-Go was the name given by the Japanese to their plan for massive air attacks on U.S. amphibious forces. The plan included Kamikazes and bombers in unprecedented numbers. Admiral Ugaki was the man in charge of Ten-Go. He decided to use a bit of a gimmick to get his suicide pilots to associate a special pride and status to their forthcoming mission. The admiral knew that the Chrysanthemum was a favored flower among the Japanese people. He decided to label his attacking aircraft Kikusui, which means, Floating Chrysanthemum. On April 6, 1945, Operation Ten-Go began. The Kikusui headed our way in big numbers, each one committed to a one way trip. The first of the Kikusui arrived at 1500 hours, 3:00 in the afternoon. Over the next five hours 200 Kikusui attacked. The concentrated aerial strike came as no surprise to Admirals Spruance and Turner and others in the high command, because communications codes had been broken. However, we on the 834 knew nothing about this intelligence information. Nor did we have any idea that the Japanese had decided to concentrate their attacks on troopships and amphibious craft because of their cargo and their vulnerability. An LST was a highly vulnerable target.

Slow, fat, bulging with an explosive cargo, and of limited firepower, an LST was a choice target for a Kikusui.

We were prepared for a Kamikaze attack, but not for the overwhelming numbers. While concentrating on one attacking airplane, another and another and another would appear. In addition, there was the "friendly fire," the gunfire from our own U.S. Navy, that put us in serious jeopardy. The 834 suffered serious damage from the guns fired from our own ships. It was not by strategy or skill that we survived the shelling from our own lads. It was plain old good luck. "Friendly Fire!" Now there is an oxymoron if there ever was one.

We had retracted from Hagushi Beach earlier that day, anchoring a short distance offshore, in the secure company of U.S. warships, ships of the line, so to speak. At 1500 we were at battle stations, Parker and myself at the 20 millimeter gun. Parker was an amazingly placid fellow. On this day his demeanor benefited everyone on the 834. In my judgment, Parker saved our ship and our lives.

That afternoon of April 6, 1945 the Japanese Kamikazes made their death dives, exploding onto or into whatever American ship became their random selection. The folly of all those airplane recognition classes back at Camp Bradford was vividly demonstrated during the Japanese attacks. The moment an airplane was sighted, every ship in the bay commenced firing and continued firing until the plane exploded in the air, crashed into the sea, or smashed into a ship. Wild, frenetic gunning by men pulling triggers aboard ships of the U.S. Navy, the so-called "Friendly Fire," cost us many lives and destroyed many of our own ships. As a Kamikaze attacked, guns from every ship tracked the airplane, blasting away with all the firepower available, oblivious to what came between them and the enemy plane, blind to the ships that came directly into their line of fire. It was as if everyone had gone crazy, become mesmerized, were intoxicated by the event. Perhaps it was sheer panic which drove the behavior. Whatever the cause, the toll was high. Three American planes were shot down that afternoon; shot down by their fellow Americans in this free-for-all shoot-out. Pilots of those planes had made the mistake of pursuing Japanese aircraft too far. Once within range, any and every airplane became cannon fodder, fair game, the enemy.

One Kamikaze singled out the LST 834 as his final destination. He came at us off the port side, guiding his airplane, a Japanese Nate I learned later, to hit the port side amidship, precisely where Parker and I were stationed. Our guns, and those of the ships around us, fired thousands of rounds at the attacking suicide pilot, but he kept on coming. It was Parker, in my opinion, who saved us all. Calmly, and with great accuracy, he poured 20mm shells into that Japanese plane. Mere seconds from smashing into the 834 the plane veered left, out of control. It passed along our port side and crashed into the sea just off our port bow. On impact the plane exploded and sank, disappearing in an instant. The 834 was officially credited with shooting down that particular plane. I unofficially credited Parker.

It was our good fortune to have avoided annihilation by the combined effort of the Kamikaze and the U.S. Navy. "Friendly fire" delivered two 40mm shells, one in the scullery, and one in the ready house at the stern of the ship. A rain of 30 caliber shells had splattered our superstructure with more of the "friendly fire." Surrounded by friends who treat you that way causes one to wonder which enemy is the more formidable. How do we protect ourselves from our compatriots?

When darkness fell, a command went out for all ships to make smoke. Those on the command ship decided that if all the ships in the bay made smoke the result would be creation of a blanket of smoke that would hover over all of us, thereby deterring further attacks by the Japanese. Our smoke-making machine was located on the stern of the ship. To my knowledge, it had never been tested. The way it performed that night would certainly suggest that the machine had never been checked out. Or could it be that those responsible for operating our smoke-making machine did not know what they were doing? Both were undoubtedly the case.

"Make smoke," Captain Bentley commanded. The same command had been issued on every ship in the bay. Smoke began emerging from the decks of all the ships…except the 834. Instead, when our machine sputtered into operation we produced flame, but no smoke. A huge flame erupted from our smoke-maker, tossing flames high into the night sky. With the flame we provided serving as a beacon light, our position must have been visible all the way to

Tokyo. Shipmates operating the smoke-maker struggled frantically to correct the catastrophe, but the machine did not respond. Flames grew in intensity with any adjustments they made. Captain Bentley was furious. He completely lost his "cool under fire" persona. "What the hell is going on back there," he bellowed. "Who is the stupid bastard running that God damn machine? Make smoke! Make smoke." No such luck, Captain. The smoke-maker just would not make smoke. We never did get that machine to work.

The Japanese did not let up. Sporadic Kamikaze attacks continued through the night, so we remained at the gun station through the night. I really appreciated Parker's companionship that night. We were never close buddies, but all of the events we shared at that 20mm gun made for a special camaraderie. It was a day and a night to remember.

Early on April 7, 1945, we were back onto Blue Beach unloading ammunition, gasoline, TNT, and a motor pool of marines that had remained aboard the 834 until requested by their superiors to come ashore. They drove their trucks down the ramp and off they went in search of their unit. A few days later we got word that the motor pool boys had been ambushed on the road and all were dead.

Japanese resistance ashore greatly intensified in the next days when they reversed their strategy. Instead of continuing to allow U.S. forces come to them, they attacked on land and at sea. American casualties mounted. Hope for an easy victory went down the tube. One extremely fortunate event saved the lives of many of us on ships in the bay. Marines, in the nick of time, took a Japanese base where crews of fifty suicide boats were making final preparations to carry out their mission. Again, we were mighty lucky. Luck, the fickle factor, was holding out in our favor.

Chapter Twenty-one
Too Much Skylarking

A wounded LST 834 left Okinawa on April 11, 1945, bound for

Saipan, one of the southern Marianna Islands. Our mission? Repair

the 834 and take on cargo for a return to Okinawa. Ships on the

perimeter of Okinawa were taking a beating, especially on April

11. Fifty-two Kamikazes attacked the picket ships as we passed

through that very day. Traveling south in open seas in the company

of several other LSTs, we were sitting ducks once again. The only

choice was to muddle along and hope for the best.

We left Okinawa without one of our two boats, the invaluable

LCVP, and one crewman. Coxswain John Penn, the irrepressible

fellow who was always up to something, had gone off by himself with the boat. No one knew where he had gone or what had happened to him. Speculation as to the what and where of John Penn ranged from an engine breakdown, to being lost in the bay, to running out of fuel, to being hit by Japanese shore batteries, to capture by the Japanese. We left Okinawa without John or the boat.

The first two days at sea passed without incident. Then, on April 13, 1945, a radio message came which shocked everyone... President Roosevelt was dead. It was unbelievable news. In my lifetime Roosevelt had always been president. It seemed that he would live forever; always as president. Later that day officers and crew gathered together on the main deck where a eulogy was given by Lieutenant Abercrombie, the executive officer. The flag was set at half-mast. We tried going back to the routines of life at sea, but the mood persisted. There was a strange silence among the men on an otherwise noisy ship. It was a very peculiar circumstance.

The ten day journey to Saipan was safe and quiet. The Japanese left us alone. Other than a constant apprehensiveness, the trip gave us an opportunity to rest our bones and psyches after the frantic days and nights at Okinawa. Weather conditions were perfect. The sea remained calm. Radar watch was routine...no problems. Captain Bentley was my constant companion in the chart room. Ostensibly, he was studying the navigation charts. Practically, he sought a place to smoke. I studied the radar and his smoking. We got along rather well, I thought. But something was bothering the captain. Maybe I bothered him for some unexplainable reason.

On the day we reached Saipan Captain Bentley threatened to throw me in the brig again. To me, the situation that did me in was much ado about nothing. But to the skipper I was in violation of a sacred Navy ritual; the raising of the Union Jack, a little blue flag with white stars. The Union Jack is to fly on a pole in the bow of the ship to indicate the ship is at anchor. I am the guy responsible for raising the Union Jack. The process is supposed to be something of a ceremony; a rather silly ceremony in my judgment. Nevertheless, as long as one is a member of the military it is necessary to conform to many absurdities, this little flag raising being but one of them. When properly executed, the ceremony goes this way. The boatswain (Tony Danapas) stands beside the anchor chain in the bow of the ship. He is armed and ready with an enormous sledge hammer. The instant the captain commands, "Drop anchor," the boatswain strikes the clamp on the anchor chain, thereby permitting the anchor and anchor chain to rattle into the sea. As the anchor splashes into the water, I am to raise the Union Jack. Simultaneously a signalman hoists the black anchor ball up the yardarm. The procedure is reversed when the anchor is raised, but one additional element makes raising the anchor a lot sexier. On the captain's command "Up Anchor," the anchor chain is slowly ratcheted back in. At first it is a slow process because the anchor is dragging along the ocean floor. Slowly, slowly...and then the anchor breaks free from the bottom and the hauling in process becomes smooth and easy. That's the moment when the sexy part happens. As the anchor breaks free from the ocean floor the boatswain mate gets to make his salty announcement. He shouts, "Anchor's Aweigh, Captain!" At that moment the signalman takes down the anchor ball and I am to lower the Union Jack. The only thing missing is for the entire crew to be on deck in dress blues singing, "Anchor's aweigh, my boys, anchor's aweigh, farewell to college joys, we sail at break of day..." and so forth. Had that happened both the captain and Danapas would have wet their pants with delight.

Adolescent logic encouraged me to make light of the Union Jack raising ceremony. After repeated occasions when I would standby with the damned flag for an hour or so waiting for the command to drop the anchor, I got into the habit of doing something else until I heard the anchor chain rattling out. Then I would wander up to the bow and run the Union Jack up its pole. Captain Bentley noticed my leisurely approach to the task. At the Saipan anchoring I paid for it. I was loafing on the boat deck very near to the captain when the anchor was dropped. Only then did I casually go down the ladder to the main deck and stroll, all too visibly, toward my flagpole in the bow. I heard the voice of Captain Bentley shouting from the conning tower, "Shannon, get that Union Jack up. On the double! Then report to me at once." Flag up, I went straight to the captain. Our meeting was brief and to the point. "Shannon, I've had enough of your skylarking and insubordination. If you ever neglect that Union Jack again you'll serve time in the brig." He turned to Ensign

Dillon. "Mr. Dillon, see that this man does fifty hours of extra duty. He'll be painting bilges instead of skylarking about."

Going down the ladder from the conning tower I pondered what was a new term, skylarking. "Now what in the world is skylarking?" I asked myself. "I'll go ask Bob Malin. He knows all about this Navy slang." Bob Malin was up in the bow, finishing up the anchor detail. He didn't even look up when I asked him about skylarking. He said, "Snuffy, the skipper is dead right. Skylarking is the way you are all of the time. You're guilty as charged. You take everything that goes on as a big joke, goofing around all the time, not taking anything seriously. Laughing and carrying on when you should be following orders. Being a damn smart ass is how you spend your days. It doesn't bother you that you don't get promoted when every other man in your division has been promoted. You'll be a seaman as long as you're in the Navy if you don't stop skylarking and get serious. It don't make no difference that you are a radarman. You can't thumb your nose at the Navy way of doing things. Skylarking is a la-de-da way of doing things."

"Malin, get serious," I said, "How can I get worked up over raising the silly little flag? And how can anyone keep from laughing at Danapas when he shouts, anchors aweigh, captain? It's a cartoon comedy. And Bob, I sure wish you hadn't hung that ridiculous Snuffy on me. Snuffy...That's awful."

Malin smiled, a smile of immense self-satisfaction. "It fits you perfectly. Laying that name on you is the best idea I ever had."

Many years passed before I read Kurt Vonnegut's delightful book, Wampeters, Foma, and Granfalloons, and found his perfect description of skylarking. He explained it this way: "Skylarking used to be a minor offense under naval regulations. What a charming crime. It means intolerable lack of seriousness." Thanks to Kurt Vonnegut I feel some measure of vindication. The skipper and Bob Malin were right, of course. I was, indeed, guilty of that intolerable lack of seriousness. So, I became the extra duty kid. Working off extra duty hours became a way of life for me. And I never did get to the point where I could take orders from someone I considered to be a dimwit. Or was I the dimwit? Whatever the case, I did an awful lot of extra duty.

171

Saipan, for us, was a pleasant surprise. Vastly different from the view of the U. S. forces that had been involved in the lengthy and bloody fighting to oust the Japanese from the place. The island had been developed by the Japanese military as their administrative outpost and they were determined to hold on to it as well as the nearby islands of Tinian and Guam. Of the fifteen islands that make up the Marianas, Guam, Saipan, and Tinian figured most significantly in World War II. The Marianas, 3500 miles west of Hawaii, have long been coveted by various Colónizers. Spain, Germany, Britain, the U. S. and Japan; each one had exploited certain of the Mariana chain of islands. Now that Saipan, Tinian and Guam were in U. S. hands we were able to go all out with air attacks on Japan. The pleasant surprise of Saipan was, for me, simply the way it was.

Chapter Twenty-two
Fifty-eight Days at Guam

We anchored at Guam, the largest island in the Mariana group,

on April 30, 1945. I did a superlative job of hoisting the Union Jack,

whipping it into place before the anchor hit bottom. It was a most

impressive performance. The Union Jack would remain up for fifty-

eight days as we waited our turn for repairs to the 834. It was another

crazy development. Gunfire from our own ships had put us out of

action. Now we waited and waited and waited for repairs to be made

to the 834, repairing the damage to our ship inflicted by gunfire

from U.S. Navy vessels. A looney tune, but no one was injured, and

Guam surely beat being at Okinawa. With no threat of attack, we had a pretty good situation at Guam. Perhaps we should have sent thank you notes to those ships with careless gunners.

It was extremely hot at Guam, but, with the tradeoffs, it was tolerable. A movie every night and regular liberty on Gab Gab Beach. Gab Gab Beach, a sandy, dusty, hot dump of a place, Guam's finest. No trees. A few quonset huts where warm beer was served. No food. Beer and basketball, those were the choices. A few beers in the boiling sun put a guy away quickly, bringing on that special treasure, sleep. We got to see a U.S.O. show with real women and a full orchestra. But the troupe was exhausted when they played Gab Gab. Those poor women shuffling around the stage in the middle of the afternoon...they tried, but they had nothing left to give. The boys in the band had no zest for the task either. Up on that stage it must have been over 100 degrees. Nevertheless, we were starved for some entertainment and the sight of a female so the show was a hit.

Mail call at last. Yes, we were at Guam long enough for several mail calls. As usual, the packages were badly mangled, but that did not matter. We ate crumbled, stale cookies and candies and relished every bite. Some fellows received lipstick sealed envelopes and others received "Dear John" notices. And me? Again, with no sweetheart back home, I got no love letter or "Dear John."

Germany surrendered on May 7, 1945. I thought the Japanese would soon call it quits, too. At Guam, Saipan, and Tinian we watched hundreds of B-29 bombers take off every evening, just before dark, all of them heading for Japan's cities. With the incessant punishment they were taking from the nightly air raids it was inconceivable that the Japanese would go it alone for much longer. Again, I was wrong.

Japanese forces began a powerful counter-offensive on Okinawa May 24, 1945. At Yontan airfield they pulled off an unbelievable raid. The airfield was secured on April 1, 1945, and had been used by American planes non-stop ever since. But the Japanese, somehow, slipped through the radar pickets and ground observers and shipboard lookouts. They successfully landed at Yontan airfield in the midst of the U.S. operation. Ten Japanese troops hopped out of that airplane, succeeded in blowing up seven U.S. planes, damaged another twenty-six planes, and destroyed 70,000 gallons of gasoline.

It was a bold, clever raid. The Japanese were definitely not finished at Okinawa.

Meanwhile, boredom set in for my mates and me on the 834 at Guam. We did not appreciate our good fortune any longer. Waiting for our turn to get repairs, life became repetitious, monotonous, unbearable. At anchor or moored alongside other LSTs, we were impatient to get on with the war. Officers invented tasks designed to keep the crew busy. It was an atmosphere in which folly was assured. Two incidents occurred that bordered on lunacy.

Gangway watch was maintained twenty-four hours a day. One of us had to stand at the gangway, the ever-present 45 caliber pistol attached to our waist, waiting for someone to try to come aboard. The only things to watch were the water snakes that were attracted by a floodlight shining down into the water. It was absolutely absurd. One night a gunner's mate became impatient when his relief did not show up at the gangway. He decided to find the missing man. That was easy enough. The guy was in his bunk, sound asleep. After wakening his replacement the guy on watch passed through the mess compartment where several crewmen were writing letters and chatting. Being a gunner's mate, he considered himself an expert on guns. Choosing to clown around a bit before returning to the gangway, he took the pistol from its holster and pointed it at each man in the mess compartment. He zeroed in on one fellow and said, "Yes, my friend, I have you in my control, don't I. I squeeze the trigger like this, and..." Certain that the pistol had no bullets, he pulled the trigger. The pistol fired. The bullet failed to hit anyone, ricocheting off the bulkhead harmlessly. The gunner's mate was incredulous. He stared at the pistol, disbelieving what he had done. He stuck the gun back into its holster, sat down and held his head in his hands. The incident was beyond comprehension. Miraculously no one was killed.

Several new men were added to our crew. One was a tall, muscular, handsome black man. He was a magnificent physical specimen. But he despised the role he was to play as "Boy" to the officers. He soon made it known that he hated being their servant. He was sullen, intense, nervous. Some crewmen quickly, too quickly, became fearful of the man. I suspect all of the officers were shivering in their boots. For some reason he and I got along real well. Maybe it is because I am such a puny little guy and he was so powerful. But when, on principle, he rebelled against his assignment as servant to the officers, his attitude was perceived as insubordinate. The Navy of World War II had no tolerance for that sort of thing. It was not long before he was thrown in the brig. The logic of that move was simply that a few days of solitary confinement would bring him in line. That logic turned out to be dead wrong. It was another dumb decision. When he got out of the brig he was ready to fight anybody and everybody. In no time he was back in the brig, this time for an indefinite stay; indefinite because he was to be taken off the 834 as soon as details and paper work could be handled.

While the man was doing time in the brig, he had Tony Danapas afraid for his life. Danapas was responsible for escorting the prisoner from the brig to the shower and the toilet. Watching Danapas sweating out that duty a couple times every day was great entertainment for the crew. Tony was shaking in his shoes. He armed himself with a pistol and a billy club. You'd think he was escorting a murderer. If that young black man had shouted "BOO!" Tony would have dropped dead in his tracks. It was not many days before the man was taken off the 834, never to be seen or heard from again. In my judgment he was a gutsy guy, a civil rights pioneer, the victim of a foul system. It was the system and those who sanctioned it that deserved punishment, not the man who rebelled against it.

Another of the new men joined our communications division. He turned out to be a real thorn in my side. For some reason he was transferred to the 834 from another ship. He was a quartermaster second class. That gave him enough rank to be above the other quartermasters. He behaved like the new horse in the pasture, determined to establish himself high in the pecking order. The guy was a big, hairy, ugly creature who perspired profusely and smelled to high heaven. Predictably, whenever he tried to tell me what to do I told him to kiss off, or something with a similar ring to it. It was not long before he reported me to division officer Dillon who demonstrated once again that he was a complete milquetoast of a fellow. Dillon soon had me before the executive officer whose chastisement reminded me of the way I was treated by the school principal when I was in the seventh grade. The only difference was that instead of culminating the verbal chastising with a beating,

Abercrombie sentenced me to another seventy-five hours of extra duty. When would I learn to take orders from someone I considered a jerk? The answer...Never.

From the dozens of ships hanging around Guam we were plucked from the bunch to be turned into a gunnery training vessel. With the war still on we would continue to function as before, but, in addition, we would be outfitted to perform gunnery training for all of the ships around us, wherever we happened to be located. Two new officers and a supply of remote controlled target planes were added to our ship. Gunnery training. Who concocted this pipe dream? One could safely speculate that the idea had been cooked up in Washington shortly after Pearl Harbor and was just now getting to the implementation stage. But why us?

More cargo, ten Marine officers, and fifty-eight enlisted men came aboard on June 10, all bound for Okinawa. Our food supply was replenished, including a supply of flour for the ship's baker. Along with the flour came a million lively passengers...Bugs. Inside those bags of flour there must have been more bugs than flour. Guam's resident bugs decided to ship out on the 834, stowaways with plenty to eat. From that day on every loaf of bread was loaded with bugs. At first we tried to pick the bugs out of the bread, but after a few days everyone succumbed to eating buggy bread. Amos set me straight. He said, "Snuffy, those bugs aren't gonna hurt you. They've been thoroughly baked. Just think of it as enriched bread. Put a little jam on it and you won't even know they are there." Amos was right again. We ate buggy bread for months.

Jankowiak was the baker. The guy was a genius. He baked great stuff even when we were bouncing around in heavy seas. He turned out a fruit cocktail pie that was sensational. Instead of a top crust he coated the pie with sugar. There must have been ten thousand calories in every slice.

En route to Okinawa we stopped at Saipan to replace the two propellers. The actual work took only one day, but we waited almost a month to get into a floating dry dock. The Marines we were transporting to Okinawa could not have been happier with the delay. Finally, on July 8, 1945, we shipped out once more for Okinawa. The next four months of 1945 were to be the most perilous of my Navy life.

Chapter Twenty-three
Japanese Surrender—New Enemies Attack

The battle for Okinawa officially ended July 2, 1945. Navy losses were enormous. It was the most costly naval operation of World War II. Sailors killed or missing, 4,900. Sailors wounded, 4,824. Ships and landing craft sunk, 30. Ships and landing craft damaged, 368. Naval aircraft lost 763. Many excellent commentaries were written about the significance of the Okinawa campaign. One of the finest was Winston Churchill's message to President Truman on June 22, 1945. He wrote:

> "The strength of will power, devotion and technical resources applied by the United States

to this task, Joined with the death struggle of the

enemy...places this battle among the most intense

and famous of military history...We make our salute

to all your troops and their commanders engaged."

Soon after the bullets stopped, our battles with nature began.

Okinawa is a favorite target for typhoons in any year, but the 1945

typhoon season turned out to be extraordinarily severe both in

the frequency and the potency of the storms. Between July 14 and

October 11 we had to ride out six typhoons. The faster ships, the

destroyers, cruisers, battleships, could out-run the storms if the path

of the typhoon was accurately determined. An LST was far too slow

to do that. Remaining at anchor in Buckner Bay at Okinawa was not

a viable option either, because the winds were so strong they would

cast the ship onto the shore, destroying it. Consequently, we were

forced to get underway and ride out the storms at sea.

The first of the typhoons kept us at sea for seven days on a wild

ride completely controlled by the whimsy of the storm. It was a total

immersion baptism, a crash course in typhoon. We rode a sea-going

bucking bronco, but we learned that our little bathtub of a ship was a survivor, an incredibly seaworthy old girl. She rode out the storm ably and got us back to Okinawa undamaged. Many ships did not make it back.

Hagushi beaches in the aftermath of the first typhoon were littered with the wreckage of U.S. ships, landing craft, and boats that were, for one reason or another, stuck in Buckner Bay. They were helpless, thrown onto the beach, broken up, strewn here and there. The violent storm had succeeded where the Japanese had failed. Understanding the potency of the storms, actually internalizing that the typhoons dominate and control the efforts of men and their vessels, was beyond most of us. Perhaps that was a good thing. It is essential to believe that you are going to make it; that your ship is going to hold together all right. Our education in such matters was to continue. The course of study was intense, accelerated and memorable.

Our missing small boat, the LCVP that failed to return before we left Okinawa for Saipan and Guam, finally came home early in the morning as soon as we returned to Okinawa. It was a calm, quiet morning between typhoons. I was standing the 0400 to 0800 gangway watch. Hardly anyone else was awake, only cooks, a radioman, a couple guys in the engine room, and the officer of the day. It was just after daylight when I saw the boat approaching. Seeing the boat was no surprise, but this one had no crew, only the coxswain. He was waving to me. Sure enough, it was John Penn, a free spirit if there ever was one. John tied up at the gangway and came aboard. "Hi Snuffy. How you been?" John had gone off with the boat more than two months ago, but greeted me as casually as he might have had he been gone only an hour or so on official business. "John," I queried, "where the hell have you been? We thought the Japs had you for sure." He answered, "No, nothing like that. I found out that a buddy of mine from back home was here at Okinawa, so I went over to visit for a little while. When I got back, the ship was gone, so I went back and stayed with my buddy until I learned you got back. Boy, am I sleepy. We had a great party last night, but I'm paying for it today. I'm gonna hit the sack for a while. A short while I imagine. I guess I'm in for it. But it was a neat time while it lasted. The boat is in good shape. No harm done as far as I'm concerned.

Gangway watch at Okinawa, packing the 45. As Fitzpatrick
advised, I never removed the gun from its holster. I didn't know
how to cock it or shoot it.

Just tell them I'm back and the boat is back." John went below to

his bunk. I logged him in, noting the time of his return and that he

had arrived with the LCVP in good shape. Two weeks later I was

required to testify at the Captain's Mast at which John was duly

examined. He got off pretty easy. I suppose the captain figured

the war would soon end and we would all be going home before

too much longer. Penn was a good sailor. What he did was only

a bit of mischief; some skylarking that backfired. Other events of

enormous significance occurred which shifted attention away from

John's escapade. Quite by accident, his timing was perfect.

Between typhoons we entertained sailors from other ships in gunnery training. Each day another ship joined us for a sail out to the open sea. Once away from the island, the miniature airplanes, the drones, were launched from our main deck. These drones became targets. After an hour or so of shooting, the exercise ceased for the day and we sailed back to our anchorage in Buckner Bay. It was the same routine every day. Of all the absurd schemes fashioned by the brains of the U.S. Navy, this gunnery idea had to rank near the top of the list. In the light of forthcoming events the procedure took on a stature of absolute lunacy.

Another typhoon took us out to sea from August 1 to 4. Then, on August 6, 1945, the first atomic bomb was exploded above the city of Hiroshima. More than 71,000 people were killed, nearly 20,000 were seriously injured, and some 171,000 people were suddenly homeless. The U.S. dropped the second atom bomb on August 9, 1945, just after 11:00 A.M., destroying the city of Nagasaki. Earlier that morning the Japanese learned that Russia had declared war on their country. How much longer will they hold out?

Nagasaki is less than 400 miles from where we were anchored at Okinawa. Hiroshima is a little further away, perhaps 500 hundred miles. Hardly anyone on the 834 knew anything about atomic bombs. There was very little comprehension of the horrible damage caused by the nuclear explosions. Was the decision to drop the two atomic bombs a wise one, a necessary one? Were the Japanese going to capitulate even if the atomic bombs had not been dropped? Was the annihilation of all those Japanese justified? One officer on the 834 would answer, "Yes! We should kill them all."

Peace came on August 10, 1945. Both sides were essentially uninformed as to the peace negotiations. Such a circumstance established conditions for one more Japanese air attack. By complete happenstance I had a ringside seat to this tragic finale of the war. It was August 12, 1945. We were anchored in Buckner Bay, Okinawa, a few hundred yards away from the battleship Pennsylvania. I was standing along the rail on the starboard side, chatting with two other fellows. We noticed a small plane coming in, lights blinking, not traveling very fast. As the plane passed by we did not notice markings of any kind. A few seconds later a bomb exploded on the fantail of the Pennsylvania. The plane then flew inland and disappeared. Twenty sailors were killed and many were wounded, Vice Admiral Oldendorf among them. The Japanese were still very much alive and active with the war.

On August 15, 1945 we received news of Japan's unconditional surrender. World War II was over at last. The celebration was noisy, gunfire going off all over the island. On the 834 it was a dry party. The skipper did not order drinks for all hands or a special feast. Nothing. I stood at the starboard rail watching an endless string of tracer bullets go into the sky. Elated shipmates threw their arms around each other, shouting, cheering, waving their arms. It was a spontaneous display that said, "Damn it guys, we made it! And now we're going home." One person was strangely aloof from the happy occasion. It was Lichek. He stood alone alongside the rail, staring down into the water; a forlorn, pensive, crestfallen figure. For some reason I walked over and stood beside him. He and I had never had a civil conversation in all the time we were aboard the 834. But at that moment I was baffled by his apparent sadness; curious to know what in the world he was pondering. I spoke to him: "Mr. Lichek, what's wrong? Are you okay?"

Without turning his head, or in any way acknowledging my presence, he said, "This is the worst thing that could have happened. There is only one solution...Kill them all."

Dumbfounded, I stood there looking at the guy. Soon I turned and walked away. When I reached the hatchway that led below I looked back at Lichek. He had not moved. While the whole world was celebrating, Lichek was despondent. Incomprehensible? Perhaps not. Everyone else on board was overjoyed because the war was over and so were our military careers. But for Lichek, the star spangled warrior, his moment on center stage was over. Now he was destined to spend the next twenty years supervising those who would polish up the handle of the big front door. With good reason, Prince Valiant had the blues.

We continued to provide gunnery training. Instead of getting orders to put all of our resources into activities relating to peace, we were directed to intensify our marksmanship training program. Most everyone getting the training would soon be civilian, never again to fire an anti-aircraft gun. No matter. Merrily we sailed

around sending target drones aloft.

Mother Nature stepped in again to break up the routine, and she

very nearly broke up the 834 once-and-for-all. On September 16,

1945 we put to sea to engage the enemy in a fight to the finish. The

enemy was a violent typhoon that fought with greater persistence and

power than a thousand Kamikazes. Not many hours out of Buckner

Bay the storm hit us head on. The night was pitch black. Raging,

merciless seas tossed the 834 about, one moment high up on the

crest of a wave, the next moment dropping fifty, sixty feet down into

the trough, slamming us against the surging sea, causing the entire

ship to shake, twist, and tremble. It was as though the 834 was alive,

writhing in pain, groaning and moaning under the punishment it was

taking. Over and over we were pummeled by the rampaging ocean.

Could the 834 hold together this time? The odds did not seem to be

in our favor. Nor did they favor other ships in the same situation.

Our radioman picked up this message: "S.O.S.   S.O.S.   S.O.S....

We are at the mercy of the sea...Our position is..." The desperate

plea came from a nearby freighter. We, too, were at the mercy of the sea, definitely in no position to come to the aid of the men on that freighter. The 834 could break apart the very next time we are thrown against the sea. The severity of the storm and our position in it made any kind of rescuing venture impossible to contemplate. One wonders whatever happened to that vessel. Reflecting on the episode reminds me of the poignancy of the Navy hymn:

> Eternal Father, strong to save
>
> Whose arm hath bound the restless wave,
>
> Who bidd'st the mighty ocean deep
>
> Its own appointed limits keep;
>
> Oh, hear us when we cry to Thee,
>
> For those in peril on the sea!

Unlike the Japanese, the malevolent typhoon could not be forced to surrender. It could scoff at all of our sophisticated killing devices, calling the contest on or off as it wished. Once the typhoon ensnared a prisoner, it taunted, terrorized, and punished, until weary of the captive. Then it would go away as abruptly as it had come. We survived. But how? Why? Thirteen LSTs were lost during World

War II to what was officially designated, perils of the sea. Between July 14 and October 11 we rode out six devastating typhoons. Thanks to those welders back at the Ambridge shipyard in Pittsburgh the LST 834 held together. The storm passed on, permitting us to return to Buckner Bay, Okinawa.

Chapter Twenty-four
Across the Inland Sea to Kure, Japan

On November 19, 1945, off we went in search of Kure, Japan.

The purpose of our going there was to involve the boys of the Navy

in honing their skills at shooting down Japanese airplanes. We were

well aware that the enemy had surrendered, but the logic of those

in command must have been that you never can tell when we will

discover (or invent) a new enemy. The two day trip from Okinawa

to the Inland Sea and then on to Kure was a remarkable experience

in terms of the natural beauty of the Inland Sea and our flirtations

with disaster.

Kure had been an important Japanese Navy base. The city is

located on the southern part of Honshu, largest island of Japan.

Once into the Inland Sea one can understand why Kure would be of such strategic importance to the Japanese Navy. It is tucked away, a natural hideaway. The Inland Sea is surrounded by mountains and dotted with picturesque fishing boats. The scenery is magnificent, but the United States Air Force had done a thorough job of laying floating mines along the southern approach to Hiroshima and Kure. Now it became our task to wend our way through the mines, concentrating on sighting them sufficiently early to avoid them and halting our progress long enough to detonate them.

Not being a shipload of particularly wise men, and having stumbled and fumbled through a good many harrowing circumstances, a sea sprinkled with floating mines was not perceived to be a serious threat. LST 834, the Pride of Pittsburgh, was a fortress impervious to damage. That bit of bravado notwithstanding, we proceeded through the Inland Sea with unusual caution and some trepidation. A slow speed was maintained in deference to the mine threat. Lookouts in the bow had plenty of time to sight and sort out whatever we were coming onto. They needed no urging from anyone to be on the alert. If we ran into a mine, the bow lookout would be a dead potato.

Kure, Japan, a city destroyed, but the trolley's still running.

For me, it was a lovely sightseeing trip. Sailing the Inland

Sea was not a straight line event. There were frequent changes in

course. Nothing extreme; merely moderate adjustments similar to

going around a curve in the road in an automobile. Each of these

adjustments introduced a new vista, a fresh landscape. The fishing

villages we passed appeared to have been untouched by U.S. bombers.

Fallout from the atom bomb at Hiroshima had undoubtedly been

detrimental to the health and well being of the people living in those

villages, but property damage did not appear to be severe.

"Mine dead ahead, Captain," the bow lookout reported. Captain

Bentley called to the wheelhouse, "Reverse engines! Emergency

back full." The man at the enunciators immediately relayed the

message to the engine room, signaling them to action. Our progress

halted. Slowly the 834 groaned into reverse. Moments later Bentley

ordered engines stopped. We floated dead in the water, silently.

There it was, a genuine U.S.A. floating mine riding gently in the

water, waiting to blow us out of the water. What an irony; a product

of the American war effort, transported across the Pacific Ocean by

the U.S. Navy, deposited in the Inland Sea by the U.S. Air Force, now threatening to destroy a ship of the U.S. Navy. We succeeded in destroying the floating mine after a number of embarrassing failures. Ultimately, Parker did the firing that succeeded. Again, he was our hero without reward. "Engines ahead, resume normal pattern," barked the captain. "Bow lookouts stay on the alert. That was a job well done."

We saw only one more mine. This one was missed by the lookout in the bow, but was sighted by those standing along the port side. The mine was far enough away to be harmless to us. It was only an accident, but a fortunate one. No effort was made to detonate the second mine. We conveniently neglected that responsibility and proceeded to Kure harbor.

Japanese islands are of volcanic origin, which produced a seemingly endless collection of excellent harbors. Kure was one of the principal shipbuilding and ship repair centers of the powerful Japanese Navy. The Yamato battleship was constructed at Kure. The Yamato and a twin, the Musashi, were the largest battleships in the world. Both are now at the bottom of the sea. The Yamato was sunk by U.S. air and surface forces off Okinawa on April 7, 1945.

The giant ship was en route to Buckner Bay, Okinawa on a suicide mission.

Kure is a harbor containing deep water coves and inlets, a perfect camouflage for hiding large ships. Ultimately the ships were discovered by U.S. bombers, and raids by American planes July 24-28, 1945 signaled the end of the Japanese Navy. Three battleships, four cruisers, five destroyers, and three carriers were scuttled by the Americans. That sight greeted us when we entered Kure Harbor. We would now share the anchorage with ships of the Japanese fleet. One difference; we were afloat, they were on the bottom. Superstructures remained visible, but the once proud warrior vessels rested on the harbor floor. Kure harbor had become a warship cemetery for the Japanese Navy.

Chapter Twenty-five
The Civility of a Conquered People

Although somewhat uneasy about mixing with the Japanese people on their own turf, getting ashore for a few hours was irresistible. Rather abruptly we were switching from killing each other to mingling, socializing with each other. In retrospect, one wonders about the powers of peaceful measures for solving world problems when compared with the brutal powers of war. No one on the 834 knew one word of the Japanese language. What makes that reality even worse is that we were rather proud of that fact. Once again, ignorance was our close companion. We compensated in typical American style; with swagger, brashness, nervous laughter, arrogance. We wore a facade that masked the fact that we were a bit scared. Surely the Japanese people were apprehensive, too. How were their "conquerors" going to treat them? They were in the unenviable position of having to accommodate this horde of men who displayed customs and manners so different from their own culture. Surely they wondered if we were going to push them around, hurt them. There was an awkwardness on both sides, which got in the way of a quick assimilation of the thoughts and ideas of each other. But a rather peculiar quest turned out to be just what was needed to dissolve all of the apprehensions of myself and my buddies, as well as those of the Japanese people who befriended us.

Bernard Minear, a shipmate and a good friend, had this crazy desire to buy a fancy Japanese dagger. I have no idea where he got such a notion. Maybe from the movies. Bernard had his mind set on buying an ornate ceremonial Japanese dagger. So, searching for such a dagger became the primary mission of our first liberty in what was left of Kure, Japan.

There was not much still standing in Kure. The U.S. bombings destroyed most everything. Our planes flew 1,747 sorties on Kure on July 24, 1945. How could anything be left of the city? A smokestack here and there, a few dwellings somehow remained in tact, trolley cars were going along the tracks just fine, some food shops were open for business. That was it. A sizable old city had become broken buildings, but the people were certainly were not broken. They were scurrying about in what appeared to be a kind of business as usual manner. And there we were, evolving a scheme to locate a dagger for Bernie.

We approached a man and his wife as they passed on the street. Communicating by way of a sign language and body language improvised on the spot, Bernard went into some silly gestures and sounds intended to get across to the astonished couple that he wanted to buy a Japanese dagger. Bernie did not get his message across, but the man, also using a language of gestures, invited the three of us to follow them. It turned out that we were invited to the couple's house, one of the few left standing, and but a short distance from where we met. Arriving at their tiny dwelling, we yielded to their sign language to remove our shoes and set them just inside the door.

I shall never forget how gentle and polite these two people were. We had unleashed the horrors of the atomic bomb on a civilian population, yet, these lovely people were gracious hosts to us. Ordinarily we behaved as noisy, pushy American sailors, not possessing much in the way of social graces. But the demeanor of our hosts had a quieting influence on us. We sat on pillows on the floor, around a small coal burning heater. Through numerous cups of tea served in delicate cups, Bernard persisted. At last the man and his wife breathed the Japanese equivalent of "Aha, I understand." The man went into another part of the house. When he returned a moment later he carried a Japanese dagger that fit Bernard's dreams to perfection. The couple insisted that it be a gift, but Bernard would have none of that. He left a generous amount of American money to the couple and , after lengthy, gracious expressions of our thanks from both sides, we left. It was a splendid first meeting with the Japanese people.

We returned to the ship in time for evening chow and excited conversations about that first liberty in Kure. Then we went topside for fresh air, but were treated to watching our mess cooks treat a Japanese man abominably. After the way we had been treated by the Japanese couple earlier in the day, it was a terrible sight. They treated the man like he was a pig, but my shipmates found the incident amusing, even entertaining. Mess cooks have a horrible job. One of their tasks is getting rid of the garbage. They must carry it to the main deck where it is then dumped over the side into a garbage scow. However, as soon as we reached Japan they discovered that starving Japanese people were eager to get the garbage and use it for their own nutritional needs. They came alongside hoping to obtain the food we were discarding. Those discarded bits of potatoes, tomatoes, bread, corn and such were life savers. Our mess cooks took advantage of the desperate circumstances of those people. I watched the mess cooks signal a Japanese man to bring his boat in close so they could dump the garbage into his boat. Actually, their objective was to coax the man in close enough so they could dump the garbage directly onto the man in the boat. They succeeded. I will never forget the sight of that poor fellow standing in his boat, garbage dripping off his face and clothing, bowing in gratitude to the mess cooks looking down at him and laughing, pleased with their accomplishment. The conquering heroes at their best? Or worst?

The same scenario was replayed over and over, wherever we anchored in Japan. The worst part, for me, is that I did nothing to stop it. Nothing! A total disregard for the dignity of another human being and I did nothing to stop it. I rationalized my behavior by telling myself that I was among the lowest ranking men on the ship, a guy with absolutely no authority. But that did not work very well. I suppose it was easy to live with the notion that the Japanese deserved whatever punishment and humiliation we chose to inflict upon them. Surely someone on our ship had the maturity and sensitivity to correct the situation. But no one did. My skylarking was considered a punishable offense, but the barbarian act of deliberately pouring garbage over a Japanese citizen whenever the opportunity came along was considered acceptable conduct meriting cheers and applause. It was a black mark on all of us.

Chapter Twenty-six
Sasebo – A City to Savor

Two weeks at Kure were quite enough. When orders came for us to move to Sasebo, Japan, we were ready to go. Sailing alone, we journeyed across the Inland Sea, into the Pacific, around the southern end of Kyushu, then northwest passed Nagasaki to Sasebo Naval Base. Nagasaki was an ugly sight. I did not feel right about our having dropped the atomic bombs. It was a merciless act, unnecessary in my judgment. Some have opinioned that the two atom bombs were dropped as a message to the Russians. If that is accurate, it is a real tragedy. Could we have had that much disregard for the Japanese?

Both the Navy base and the city of Sasebo were in pretty good shape. The natural surroundings were right out of a picture book illustrating the idyllic locations of Japan. Hillsides were extensively developed into vegetable gardens. The climate was favorable for cultivating both food and people. Whether by deliberate strategy or good fortune, the Navy base was fully functioning. Buildings, piers, dry-docks, roadways; all were ready for use by the United States Navy. It was my good fortune to be at Sasebo for three months, December 15, 1945, to March 14, 1946.

The island of Kyushu is almost tropical. A mild climate and good soil mean three crops a year. Put that together with abundant seafood and liberty in Sasebo became first rate. Just wandering the streets sipping sake from a tall green bottle, or gorging on locally grown mandarin oranges, was fine duty. Top the day off with a few hours in one of the natural hot springs and a liberty became a genuine rest and recreation occasion. The three months at Sasebo were congenial times; pleasant, relaxing, and fun. The pressures were off. Anxieties and tensions associated with war and all the aspects of a kill or be killed endeavor were long gone. Another enormous bonus was that we could literally count the days and make some reasonable projections on when we would leave the 834 for good. The prospect of returning to the United States and starting an entirely new set of possibilities in life made for the good life while in Sasebo. Like most everyone else, I started to focus on my tomorrows.

Soon after the war ended I got permission to convert our tank deck into a basketball court. The shipfitters put their talent and equipment to the task, welding support beams and constructing the four by six foot backboards. Balls and baskets were requisitioned on the Navy base and we were ready to play ball. Not great, but an arena where many, many basketball games were played. Games pitting the 834 team against teams from other ships became the number one activity for some of the crew; especially me. Then at Sasebo we really struck it rich. We found a full length basketball court on the third floor of a building only a short walk from where the 834 was moored. Compared to the limitations of our shipboard court, the Japanese facility seemed as grand as Madison Square Garden. Our basketball program really flourished in that setting.

Basketball converted me into a commissioned officer for one evening. For two hours the sow's ear (me) became a silk purse. Someone had arranged a game between our commissioned officers and those of a destroyer anchored nearby. The best player among our officers was Bob Latz. He had been a college star. He knew the game well, with good moves, great anticipation, a good shooter and rebounder. Latz made things happen on the basketball court and everywhere else. But things he made happen during the afternoon prior to the scheduled game took him out of the lineup with a smile on his face. Bob Latz had gone ashore for what turned out to be a marvelous party. When he returned to the ship that evening he was in high spirits, but in no way able to take his place in the basketball game. That is when Captain Bentley waved his magic wand and made me an officer for the basketball game. In an instant everyone of our commissioned officers became my peers, my teammates. I replaced Bob Latz on the officer's basketball team. I played well, had a good game. We won. We shook hands all around. The officers from the destroyer retired to the officer's wardroom for drinks and socializing with officers of the 834. One officer missed out on the party in the wardroom…Me. I returned to being CinderBob. The skipper sent me two cans of beer and his thanks. Bernard Minear drank one beer and I drank the other. Still in the mood for celebrating, I drank a highball consisting of 180 proof medical alcohol mixed with orange juice, courtesy of the pharmacist mate. I finished off the evening and myself with a few swigs of Parade after-shave lotion. My shipmates assured me that Parade's high alcohol content made it okay to drink. Boy, was that a mistake. I soon felt I had turned as green as the after-shave lotion. The next day I was a walking disaster. But, thanks to Bob Latz and his afternoon party, I had escaped my status at the bottom of the pecking order, became a commissioned officer, performed well, and was showered with accolades from my shipmates.

Chapter Twenty-seven
Back on the Perilous Edge

A note received March 14, 1946 directed us to proceed at once

to Yokosuka, Japan. Theoretically, this was an easy assignment.

Simply travel south around the tip of Kyushu, then sail directly

north into Tokyo Bay and the port city of Yokosuka on the island

of Honshu. Everything went well until we reached Tokyo Bay.

Suddenly we were smothered by a fog so dense that visual navigation

was impossible. Not to worry, radar can do the job. Shipping lanes

going in and out of Tokyo Bay were jammed with ships from all over

the world, but those ships were seen only as dots on the radar screen.

We were getting along just fine, maintaining an accurate fix on ships

ahead and behind. Suddenly the radar went dead. In an instant we had gone blind. Radar stopped without a warning of any kind. Blasts from foghorns were incessant, but we had no way of knowing where they came from or which direction the ships were traveling. The sound of a foghorn is always an ominous moaning. Engulfed by the foghorn blasts it seemed that ships were bearing down on us from every direction. Approaching ships had no way of knowing that LST 834 was a loose cannon.

I turned off the power and removed the metal case which covered the radar. From that point on I was useless. Our division officer stood beside us, but he was equally useless. Amos took charge. Excellent Amos, cool and unperturbed, peered into the maze of tubes and electronic circuitry. His diagnosis of the problem was swift, efficient, and accurate. After a quick referral to the radar manual to confirm what he thought was the solution to the problem, Amos replaced a tube. We reassembled the unit, pushed the power button, and the radar came back to life. And none too soon. I notified the skipper that a ship was dead ahead and closing fast. He responded by ordering an immediate turn to starboard, thereby averting a collision. A huge Japanese tanker slid by us on the port side, so close that we could have reached out and touched it. Radar had saved us. Amos had saved us. His unflappable performance was our salvation.

The dense fog and a near collision put Captain Bentley in a state of nervous exhaustion. He had had enough. He popped into the navigation room and examined the chart to make certain of our position in Tokyo Bay. Satisfied that we would be safe if we left the channel, he ordered a turn to starboard that took us out of the traffic. Radar revealed that no ships were moving in our direction. That should have given someone pause to wonder why, but it didn't. Indeed, ignorance was bliss. Judging that we were in a safe zone, Captain Bentley put the anchor detail to work. In a few minutes we were anchored somewhere in Tokyo Bay. The 834 rested quietly that night. So did the captain and crew.

By mid-morning the fog had disappeared. It was clear skies over Tokyo Bay. Then came news from the U.S. ship in charge of affairs in that section of Tokyo Bay telling us that we had moved through and were anchored in a restricted mine field. It was a reckless, stupid blunder by the captain, unnecessarily placing every one of us in harm's way. From Captain Bentley's perspective, the decisions he had made without seeking any instructions or clarifications were in everyone's best interest, especially his own. This was to be his final voyage aboard the 834. At Yokosuka he was to be relieved of command, freed from the duties he found so distressing. Why, he must have said to himself, should I risk an ignominious demise in the fog of Tokyo Bay, only a few miles, a few minutes, from my last port of call? It was perfectly understandable logic. Who could fault his decision? We did not strike a mine, we escaped the fog and no one was injured. Now we proceed across the bay to Yokosuka. Captain Bentley was ecstatic. He even came through the chart room singing: "I'd rather be me than someone else that I know." And who is that someone else who will replace him as Captain? That is the critical question on everyone's mind.

At Yokosuka we were overwhelmed by a flurry of activity. It was a wild scene, as two fuel tankers, a fresh water tanker, a garbage scow, and a boat removing those damned radio controlled drones attached themselves to the 834. Adding to the frenzy were the sights I could see from our boat deck. Mount Fujiyama looked to be just down the road, but the snow-capped peak was seventy miles away.

Anchored nearby was the battleship Iowa, a real beauty of a ship.

And the 834 setting in Tokyo Bay, an ocean in itself. They were

spectacular sights to behold.

Chapter Twenty-eight
Tokyo – Where Two Emperors Reign

By 1:00 in the afternoon of a lovely spring day, 1946, I was

on a train for Tokyo with two of my shipmates. The train was

comfortable, inexpensive, fast, and on time. What was especially

noteworthy is that this fine train service was on a railroad that had

been bombed over and over, every night for many months. Somehow

the Japanese kept the line functioning. Oddly enough, we were now

the beneficiaries of their resourcefulness. As the train approached

Tokyo the gruesome consequences of nightly B-29 raids became the

scenery. Mile after mile of bombed out landscape as far as the eye

could see. Our firebombs had wiped out everything. In the first

six hours of the March firebombing of Tokyo, more people were killed than at any other time in the history of mankind. Fifteen square miles of Tokyo were destroyed in one night. The firebombing continued in relentless fashion, night after night, until the Japanese agreed to an unconditional surrender. By the end of May, according to Japanese documents, the homes of 2,726,000 people in Tokyo had been destroyed. It was the civilian population that paid the bill for the determination and tenacity of the Japanese military leadership.

In spite of the destruction of the city, we were in for some pleasant surprises and a great liberty in Tokyo. Coming in on the train we talked with some sailors who had done Tokyo several times. They gave us a run down on what to look for, where to go, and what to see. They surprised us with one announcement: "Expand the two B's essential in a good liberty town to three." Yes, they agreed on booze and brothels, but the third one, Burgers, was the bonus. A center similar to a U.S.O. had been established and they served BURGERS every day. It was a kind of peculiar thing to get excited about maybe. Nonetheless, discovering real American hamburgers was a discovery better than gold. Tokyo would be a winner.

Outside Tokyo's central train station rickshaws and their drivers were lined up waiting for customers. Each of us engaged a rickshaw. I climbed into mine and leaned back, just like I knew what I was doing. Before the operator could get hold of the long handles of the vehicle I upset the rickshaw, tipping it backwards, crashing it to the pavement. I ended up on my back, looking up into the afternoon sky over Tokyo and looking at the handles of the rickshaw that were perpendicular to the street rather than parallel to the street. I was not hurt. A bit befuddled, but not hurt. We all got a good laugh out of my predicament, but the poor guy who piloted the rickshaw was scared and apologetic. I tried to assure him that I was all right, that I was OK. Fortunately, OK had become a part of his vocabulary somewhere along the line. It is a magic word. I accepted whatever he was saying in what seemed to be an apology. Who knows, he might have been saying, "You jerk, how could you do anything so stupid?" Off we went, riding like royalty, three sailors rolling along the streets of Tokyo in rickshaws.

But where to? I shouted to Bernard Minear, "Hey Bernie, let's go have a look at the Imperial Palace." That sounded good to him and our buddy. The rickshaw pilots seemed to understand. They nodded, indicating that they got the message. We relaxed and enjoyed the journey to the palace of Emperor Hirohito. The route was downright pastoral. Lovely trees and grass and shrubbery. No congestion in the area. Plenty of open space. Now and then an American automobile of pre-war vintage passed by, transporting some Japanese business executive or political hotshot or high ranking U.S. military dignitary to who knows where.

Touring Tokyo in rickshaws

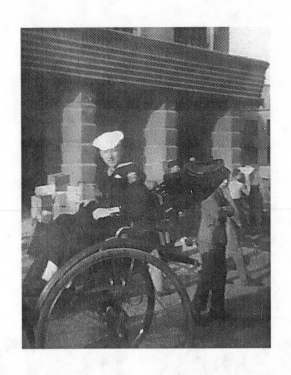

At the Emperor's Palace, Tokyo

Tokyo

Robert Shannon

ロバート シヤノン.

A Japanese artist did this sketch in Tokyo

The cars appeared to be in excellent condition. Clearly, they had received tender loving care during the war years. The presence of a 1940 model of Buick, Chrysler, or Lincoln on the streets of Tokyo immediately after the war struck me as quite an incongruity. In retrospect, their presence should not have been a surprise. Trade between the United States and Japan had certainly been extensive before the war. But seeing an American auto that was not a military vehicle was cause for celebration. It was a taste of home for guys who were really starving for it.

At the gates of the Imperial Palace we settled with the rickshaw drivers and they hustled off in search of the next passengers. We walked as close as we could get to the palace grounds, gawking like the small town Midwest hicks we were. It was an impressive scene; awesome for a kid like me who was as culture bound as a person can be. A Japanese university student with a camera had set up a little business just outside the gates to the palace. He spoke English very well, proposing to do a photo of the three of us standing in that royal setting. With nothing to lose but the few yen he charged, we agreed to his proposition. He took our names and stateside addresses. Sure enough, the fellow was completely trustworthy. The photograph arrived, just as he had promised, a delightful piece of memorabilia.

An enterprising student artist was doing charcoal sketches of passers by. I sat for a portrait. It turned out to be a remarkable characterization. Perhaps more of a caricature than a characterization. Anyway, it was fun to do, and it introduced us to another English speaking Japanese person. I asked him if he had any idea where General MacArthur had his headquarters. He did, indeed, and was happy to explain how to find the building. It was only a short walk from where we stood. Great! Let's have a look.

Emperor MacArthur's headquarters, Tokyo

General MacArthur, the second of the two emperors living in Tokyo, had set himself up in royal style. President Truman blessed MacArthur with the lofty title, Supreme Allied Commander. Playing to this grand status, MacArthur commandeered one of the few buildings in Tokyo to withstand the bombings. It had been headquarters for a large insurance company, but, as they say, "To the victor go the spoils." Once MacArthur took over the place the Japanese people referred to it as the Dai Ichi building. Dai Ichi means Number One. I believe MacArthur suffered from sovereign envy. One wonders how he resisted the temptation of moving into the Imperial Palace. Perhaps the building he chose was far better. A long reflecting pool created an extremely impressive approach to the Dai Ichi building. In a "what do we have to lose" frame of mind we entered the general's building, punched the Otis elevator button for the top floor, and up we went. In a moment we stood in the reception room of the Supreme Allied Commander. That's as close as we got to MacArthur. Good enough. We did learn that MacArthur could see the Imperial Palace from his lofty perch atop the Dai Ichi building. Otis returned us to the ground level and our exploration of Tokyo continued.

In a more congested section of the city that looked as though it had been an area of up-scale boutiques and smart shops for Tokyo's chic, we came upon a somewhat startling surprise...The Ernie Pyle Theater. Someone, somehow, in the hierarchy of the American occupation force, had arranged for a fine theater building that had survived the firebombings to be renamed, The Ernie Pyle Theater, in honor of the American journalist killed on Okinawa. We went inside the theater and settled into a terrific show. Japanese artists in colorful costumes displaying extraordinary talents; acrobats, jugglers, dancers, and a live band, put on a wonderful show.

After the theater we nosed around in search of a place to eat. Good fortune was ours. We happened onto the Imperial Hotel. The internationally acclaimed hotel was beyond our financial and social status. Nevertheless, we decided on one of those throw caution to the wind splurges and treated ourselves to a fine meal in a sumptuous setting. No mess trays, no chow line, no garbage cans. It was a thoroughly civilized dinner, with table cloth, napkins, plates, glasses, silverware, wine, delicious food, excellent service, and live music. And we survived the bill.

"Now what?" Bernard asked. "It's only eight o'clock. Too early to catch the train back to Yokosuka."

I said, "How about a Geisha House, like those guys on the train told us about?" Agreed, we found one, an upstairs place that was a knock-out. Gorgeous girls treated us to a grand entertainment and continuous tea served in tiny cups throughout the evening. It was a fantastic place. Such a short time had passed since we were engaged in annihilating these lovely women by any means at our disposal. Sheer madness on both sides.

I was able to return to Tokyo many times, always for a fine experience. But there were so many things I did not do simply because of my ignorance and my mid-American mind set. I squandered so many opportunities in Tokyo because I had no vision of the possible. The smug, conquering hero mentality intruded, too. The Japanese people were remarkably friendly and helpful. I was never aware of any animosity or hatred of us on the part of any civilian I met. But instead of finding out as much as possible about the Japanese culture, I focused my attention on counting my points and calculating how soon I would have enough to go home. Leaving Japan would be fine, but far more important to me was the day I would leave the 834 behind. As shipmates we had had more than enough of each other. With the end of my Navy days in sight, I figured that learning about other cultures could wait. That was another unfortunate generalization on my part.

Bob Latz, our new skipper, was an excellent choice to replace Bentley.

Chapter Twenty-nine
China – End of the Line at Last

One more port of call before I bid farewell to the 834 and my shipmates. The voyage from Yokosuka, Japan to Tsingtao, China was, in some respects, a sentimental journey. Ironically, we departed Japan on April 1, 1946, one year to the day from the Easter Sunday invasion of Okinawa. Now, with most of the world adjusting to some brand of peace, there was a spirit of optimism, a sense of relief, an anticipation of good things about to happen in my life. Another factor influencing my mood was the absence of Captain Bentley and the presence of Captain Latz. Bentley was gone forever, relieved of duty on the 834. The man was on his way home. Shortly before his departure, Captain Bentley appointed Bob Latz as his replacement.

To me and to most everyone in the crew, Bob Latz, now Captain Latz, was a wise and popular choice. It was not that he knew much about the manifold tasks and operational elements basic to making the ship and ship's company function. What he did know is which men among the officers and crew had the expertise, the knowledge of particular aspects of the ship's operation. Bob was good with people. The atmosphere aboard ship had changed in a positive way when Bentley left and Captain Latz took over. There was a shift from a threat dominated mode of leadership to one based on cooperative interaction. Captain Latz had no pretensions. He knew he was operating by the seat of his pants, but that was okay. Bob Latz was the kind of fellow others rally round. Everyone wanted the new skipper to succeed. And he did.

Spirits were good. There was no scowling, except from Lichek. He managed to sustain his "Ain't it awful" countenance. Perhaps he thought he should have been named captain. What a disaster that would have been. He would have outdone Captain Bligh. Indeed, his continuing grumpiness was a surprise to no one. He had nothing to cheer about in his future, nothing to look forward to but years and years in the Navy. Poor fellow. Soon after arriving in China he would be left behind with the 834 and a fresh batch of seamen to instruct in "polishing the handle so carefully." Thirty of us in the original crew were scheduled to escape from the 834 on April 15, 1946. Some poor soul would become my replacement as Lichek's favorite whipping boy. Whoever he is, he will have a tough time topping my incorrigibility record. It is probable that my sparkling career as Lichek's lament remained unsurpassed.

Six days at sea put us off the coast of China in a bit of a quandary. Captain Latz was in the conning tower with my division officer, now Lieutenant Dillon after his automatic promotion for having served eighteen months as an ensign. Navigation lights onshore had the new skipper confused as to where we were. Dillon, always confused, was of no help. Knowing our exact position was imperative in order to set a course that would take us into Tsingtao Harbor. Latz and Dillon came down to the navigation room to study the chart and to have a look at what I was seeing on the radar screen. From my perspective, radar revealed quite clearly a shoreline configuration that corresponded with points on the chart where onshore navigation lights were located. Dillon confidently explained what we needed to do to make it into the harbor. His idea was at odds with mine, but my opinion had not been sought. Captain Latz then asked for that second opinion...mine. With the new skipper and Dillon looking over my shoulder, I explained what I considered to be the salient features of what appeared on the radar screen and transposed those radar marks to the navigation chart. Captain Latz reflected on what I had said, weighing it against what Dillon had advocated. He said, "You know, I'm inclined to think Bob is right. We'll proceed into the harbor following his guidelines. Come on, Joe. Let's get back up there and we'll be underway in no time." The two men returned to the conning tower where Captain Latz set a course following my suggestions. I was right. We had no trouble sailing to our designated anchorage in Tsingtao Harbor.

As soon as the anchor detail had been secured I shut down the radar. It was to be my final radar watch on the 834. My career as a radarman was over. It was certainly not a distinguished career, but I never got the ship in any trouble. We were involved in a good many predicaments where radar was critically important, too. Making a vital contribution into getting us on the right path to Tsingtao Harbor was a gratifying wind up to that segment of my life devoted to reading and interpreting the radar screen. Now to raise that damned Union Jack for the last time.

Next morning our sea bags came out of storage. Although it was a simple procedure, getting my hands on that old sea bag was of tremendous symbolic significance. It was April 8, 1946, seven full days before I would leave the 834 and board a troop ship for the trip home, but a guy has to have time to pack. Actually, seven minutes would have been plenty of time to throw my limited possessions into that bag and say goodbye to the 834. But getting the seabag out of storage, seeing my name boldly stenciled on it, stuffing it under my mattress, knowing that it was standing by ready and waiting... extremely important stuff.

Since November 4, 1944, the LST 834 had set the parameters for my shipmates and me. We were arbitrarily placed on this steel island 327 feet long and 50 feet wide and obligated to establish an all male society that would live (and possibly die) together. The term of our confinement was vaguely defined as the war's end and six months.

One hundred fifteen men, heretofore unknown to each other, to the ship, to life at sea, or to the tasks they would be expected to perform, were abruptly bundled onto the new ship and told to go to it. The subsequent social structure that emerged was the antithesis of what any of us had previously known.

It has always seemed paradoxical to me that those who went off to fight a war for our brand of democracy were required to adapt to living in an autocratic, top-down, hierarchical social structure. A basic principle of that social structure being that there are those who command and those who are commanded. The assumption is that democracy will not work in the military. Those who choose a career in the military would no doubt agree with such an assumption. But, based on my experience on the LST 834, I emphatically reject such an assumption. In my opinion, our operations would have functioned far more effectively under the principles of democracy. Surely there were some exemplary ship captains who conducted the ship's business with a style that complemented the values of the society. In those situations where the shipboard society is a participatory democracy, I believe morale would be high and the mission successful. Not so on the 834. It was a ship where the prevailing doctrine was that of the commanding and the commanded. The consequence was an allegiance of the commanded to a tight knit sub-culture which developed a strong, powerful interdependency. Even those among the commanded who disliked each other managed to cooperate with each other. This sub-culture was indispensable to make life endurable for the commanded. Now that we were but a few days from the termination of our existence as shipmates, everyone was amiable, friendly. Old so-and-so was not such a bad guy after all. It was the sub-culture operating again. There was a tendency to believe that something would go wrong with our dream of going home. We needed each other to keep the dream alive. It was a peculiar syndrome.

Whether it was good planning, divine providence, or a lucky punch, Tsingtao, China turned out to be a marvelous place to wind up my career as a sailor. It was a pleasant happenstance. Tsingtao, before the war, had been a popular resort city. Most of the people living there were, of course, Chinese. But we discovered a conspicuous number of people in the city who were German; settlers

234

who had gravitated to Tsingtao because of the enticing economic opportunities. These people had prospered. A German brewery produced the world-renowned beer bearing the city's name, Tsingtao Beer. It was a German beer produced in China by Germans. A large Catholic cathedral dominated a busy intersection in the city center. The cathedral was a consequence of the German population living in Tsingtao. There was a German dairy doing a fabulous business. Evidence of the German influence was on every street corner. And Russians, too, had found Tsingtao a place to prosper. They were referred to as White Russians. I wondered why the Germans were not labeled White Germans?

Huge economic disparities existed among the Chinese in Tsingtao. Beggars were everywhere, especially children. They were good at their job, too. Disarming little kids swarmed around us in the streets and on the pier. The money they collected represented a huge boost in family income. The beggars were a pitiful side of life in Tsingtao.

April 15, 1946, the glorious day that I and twenty-nine shipmates had so long awaited, took an unbelievably ruinous turn of events when the officers demanded a last minute seabag inspection. It was incredible, absolutely incredible. What should have been an occasion when officers would express their gratitude and good wishes to those of us from the original crew, turned into a final show of distrust. All of us who were heading home had assembled near the gangway ladder with our carefully packed seabags. We were ready! The boat was standing by, ready to transport us to the Monrovia, the troopship across the harbor that would take us home. Understandably, there was a considerable amount of nervousness and impatience. The feeling that something might go wrong was still present. Sure enough, something did go wrong.

One of the officers had discovered that a supply of new foul weather jackets was missing. Once he got word to the other officers that their new jackets were missing they quickly surmised that we had them in our seabags. We were subjected to an inspection then and there on the main deck. Our division officer looked on while I emptied my bag onto the deck. Not one of the foul weather jackets was discovered. Not one of the officers apologized for their greedy suspicions. Now to re-pack the seabag. The first packing had been done in meticulous fashion, arranging things carefully for the long voyage home. After the intrusive, degrading inspection I crammed my belongings back in the bag, tied a line to it and lowered it down into the boat. I want to believe that Captain Latz knew nothing of the disgusting scheme we had just experienced. It smelled like something Lichek would cook up in response to a report from a guy like Broadbent, the goodies provider. It was one more kick in the pants for a going away present; one more demonstration that crewmen were considered lesser beings subject to the whimsical, capricious notions of a "superior" officer. The seabag inspection was appropriate in that it was so characteristic of my life on LST 834. But the contempt it generated would last me a lifetime.

Following that bitter anti-climax we were at last permitted to go down the ladder and into the LCVP for our last ride in the small boat. There was no looking back, no wave of farewell. But we were in need of something that would put us in better spirits. Here we were heading home and we were all pissed off. Our new boat crew had the solution. Halfway to the Monrovia two members of the boat crew pulled a large carton from under a canvas at the stern. They brought the box into the well of the boat and ripped it open. There they were, the foul weather jackets the officers were seeking. The new boat crew had gladly agreed to be accomplices in the coat scam. But who master-minded the deal? I never learned who he was. The supply of jackets was quickly distributed among my shipmates and the empty carton tossed into the sea. I stuffed one of the contraband coats into my seabag. It was an emblem signifying another small victory of the commanded over those who command.

The Monrovia sailed from Tsingtao, China on April 15, 1946. We passed by the 834, close enough to hear the call, "Now hear this…" Indeed, I had heard this for the last time. Goodbye, old girl. Yes, I will miss you, but oh so gladly. I watched her disappear from my sight and my life. But she, too, returned to the United States; this time for burial. She was decommissioned September 12, 1946, struck from the Navy list October 8, 1946, and sold to Kaiser Company Incorporated, Seattle, Washington for scrapping in December, 1947. With her one battle star, she died.

Acknowledgments

Many books and monographs were helpful in verifying accuracy

and adding detail to events I have written about in this memoir. They

are: *Kamikazes and the Okinawa Campaign*, U. S. Naval Institute

Proceedings (1954); *Who Were the Kamikazes?* U. S. Naval Institute

Proceedings (1957); *A Boy's War*, Paxton Davis (1990); *Hirohito, the*

War Years, Paul Manning (1986); *Okinawa, the Last Battle of World*

War II, Robert Leckie (1995); *Hiroshima and Nagasaki*, R. G. Grant

(1998); *The Battle for Okinawa: A Japanese Officer's Account of the*

Last Great Campaign of World War II, Colonel Hiromichi Yahara

(1995); *History of United States Naval Operations in World War II*,

Samuel Eliot Morison, Volumes VIII (1964) and XIV (1960); *Victory*

In the Pacific, Samuel Eliot Morison (1945); *Okinawa: Victory In the*

Pacific, Charles Nichols and Henry Shaw (1955); *All the World's Fighting Ships 1922-1946*, Roger Chesneau, Editor (1980); *Typhoon of Steel*, James and William Belote (1970); *Operation Iceberg: The Invasion and Conquest of Okinawa in World War II*, Gerald Astor (1995); *Beneath the Eagle's Wings: Americans in Occupied Japan*, John Curtis Perry (1980).

USS LST 834
c/o Fleet Post Office
San Francisco,
Calif.

19 June 1945

Mr. Grover Shannon
3730 Piqua Street
Fort Wayne, Indiana

Dear Mr. Shannon:

I am very proud to inform you that your son participated
in the initial invasion of Okinawa Shima, aboard this ship and
conducted himself according to the highest traditions of the
United States Navy.

I am most happy to have your son as a shipmate.

R. J. BENTLEY
Commanding, LST 834

<u>ROBERT L. SHANNON</u>

To you who answered the call of your country and served in its Armed Forces to bring about the total defeat of the enemy, I extend the heartfelt thanks of a grateful Nation. As one of the Nation's finest, you undertook the most severe task one can be called upon to perform. Because you demonstrated the fortitude, resourcefulness and calm judgment necessary to carry out that task, we now look to you for leadership and example in further exalting our country in peace.

Harry Truman

THE WHITE HOUSE

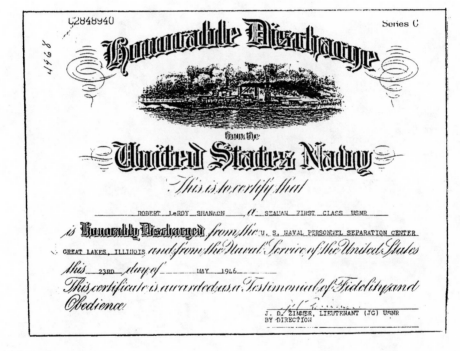

C2848940   Series C

Honorable Discharge

from the

United States Navy

This is to certify that

_____ROBERT __LeROY__ SHANNON_____ *a* __ SEAMAN FIRST CLASS USNR__

is **Honorably Discharged** *from the* U. S. NAVAL PERSONNEL SEPARATION CENTER

GREAT LAKES, ILLINOIS *and from the Naval Service of the United States*

this __23RD__ *day of* _____ MAY 1946_____

This certificate is awarded as a Testimonial of Fidelity and Obedience.

J. D. ZIMMER, LIEUTENANT (JG) USNR
BY DIRECTION